Intercede: Saints for Concerning Occasions

by

Jennifer Clark

UNSOLICITED
PRESS

Through a Project Grant for Artists, the writing of this book was supported in part by the Nevada Arts Council and the National Endowment for the Arts.

For information contact:
Unsolicited Press
Portland, Oregon
www.unsolicitedpress.com
orders@unsolicitedpress.com
619-354-8005

Cover Design: Kathryn Gerhardt
Editor: Summer Stewart
ISBN: 978-1-963115-39-0

To my mother, Nancy Engemann, who often told us she married a saint.

CONTENTS

Intercede: Saints for Concerning Occasions

DEAR READER,

Saints of all kinds wait for you within this book.

Saints are known for performing miracles and amazing feats. In their biographies of the saints, hagiographers have recorded these astonishing acts down through the centuries. However, my hope for this collection is that it pulls back the curtains heavy with miracles and feats and allows the person behind the title of "Saint" to step forth. When we can momentarily suspend our understanding of how we believe the world works and set aside our awe or skepticism, I believe we can come to a quieter, deeper truth.

We discover people who are surprisingly like us, imperfect creatures of all shades, shapes, and sizes. At times, despite their best efforts, saints fail and flounder. Some can be crotchety, dour, annoying, and humorless. Others are kind, brilliant, gentle, and downright funny. One thing they never are, however, is boring.

The writer Phyliss McGinley said that saints differ from us in their exuberance. "Moderation," she writes in *Saint Watching*, "is not their secret. It is in the wildness of their dreams, the desperate vitality of their ambitions" that sets them apart from the rest of us." I agree with these sentiments, though if you had asked me before I started on my seven-year journey of studying the saints, I would have told you that ambition is a term reserved for businesspeople and high-powered lawyers. But saints, I have learned, are exceedingly ambitious. They don't aspire to wealth or fame or attempt to amass earthly possessions. Instead, saints strive to know and be close to God. As you'll soon discover, how they choose to pursue this ambition varies from century to century and saint to saint.

Within *Intercede*, you'll meet ancient holy people like Drogo. (Born in 1105, he died 50 years before the papacy took over the

10

canonization process.) These early saints were determined to be saints based on public acclaim, what is known as *vox populi*, the "voice of the people." A number of the saints in this book have acquired their "Saint" title by going through the official canonization process of the Roman Catholic Church. And a few, in earlier stages of this process, are deemed either "Venerable," or "Blessed." You'll also meet a couple of saints, like Ursula and Wilgefortis, who never lived, though their lack of existence didn't stop their legends from being a force in this world.

I've come to believe that you, dear reader, and I are called to be part of this communion of saints. As one of my favorite saints, Mother Teresa of Calcutta, once said, "Holiness is not something extraordinary, not something for only a few brains, with intellectual powers that can reason, that can discuss, that can have long talks and read very wonderful books. Holiness is for every one of us as a simple duty – the acceptance of God with a smile, at all times, anywhere and everywhere."

Saints lead us to interesting places; often places we would never go alone. Saints shake us out of our comfort zone and plunge us into strange and foreign—but always sacred—landscapes that give us an opportunity to glimpse the Holy. In this sacred vista, we can wander alongside the saints, see that the shape of their lives, and sometimes their very bodies, are arrows pointing toward God.

Let's turn the page and see where the saints take us.

PS. It bums me out when I get to the end of a book and realize there are notes. I often like to read the note and then re-read the poem, essay, or chapter I've just read. So that's why I'm telling you this upfront: I've included notes at the back of this book that accompany many of the poems.

Connie Pan, another person besides me who welcomes notes at the end of poetry collections (I only know this because I read her essay,

"In Appreciation of the 'Notes' section in Poetry Collections" that was published October 31, 2022 in *Book Riot*), writes that sometimes the notes in poetry books "sound like poems. Sometimes they sound like essays. Sometimes they sound like brain-wrinkling facts. Notes can divulge a wide range of insights and elaborations." That, I think, aptly describes my notes, but you can decide yourself.

PPS. Okay, now you can turn the page.

"When we are who we are called to be, we will set the world ablaze."

St. Catherine of Siena (1347–1380)

Bartolomeo Bulgarini (Italian, c. 1300-1378)
"Saint Catherine of Alexandria"
Tempera on panel (c. 1335/1340)
Samuel H. Kress Collection, Courtesy of the National
Gallery of Art, Washington

LINEN WOMEN, WITH A NOD TO ST. CATHERINE OF ALEXANDRIA, PATRON SAINT OF SEAMSTRESSES

We are made for summer. Stronger wet
than dry, as hot and humid descend, we
resist carpet beetles and fungus-fed men,
and, like Catherine, refuse to shrink
from the sun. We'll remain cool before
emperors, call out their puckered thinking,
refuse to slip into their broken, biased,
stitching.

Let Spirit steam our hard
to reach places, round plackets
and pockets and buttoned collars. We
press into this wrinkled life and stretch.

Designed for the long or short trip—
no one knows which—we permit
the hand-stitched hat that's been packed
to complement each woman. Some of us boast
floppy brims, others trimmed with grosgrain
ribbon, each style crushable, able to roll
and travel.

Despite hours of iron, we soon crumple.
Come forth, well-worn ones,
for the linen maker knows each crease
and calls us to the light, rumpled, woven.

PATRON SAINT OF COOKS AND COMEDIANS

A saint walks into a bar packing a punchline.
It's 258 A.D. and Saint Lawrence's friends' heads
are rolling in the aisles—including Pope St. Sixtus II.

The opener, Rome, is just warming up
and tells Lawrence to hand over the riches
or else he'll suffer a similar fate.

As deacon, Lawrence considers the poor
his main audience. Always one for timing,
he asks for three days and Rome lets him go.

He improvises and sends the Holy Grail to his parents,
sells sacred vessels to swell the sum, and ennobles
the needy, entrusting them with the Church's wealth.

For his final sketch, Lawrence gathers the widowed,
the orphaned, and poor. "Here are the treasures
of the Church," he tells them. His delivery flawless,

Rome roasts him on a gridiron. Rome thought it killed,
but it is really Lawrence, on fire with Christ, who kills
that night. His closing line is perfect. "This side's done,"
he quips. "Turn me over and take a bite."

THE LOST ART OF PLAYING THE FOOL

Like Saint Simeon, to goad people to God,
you must first leave the desert of what you know.

Enter a town of cross-loving people and announce your new self
by leashing a dead dog to your waist, dragging the carcass down
    the street.

Give up fasting and leap into the lap of a hungry God.
Chew camel meat on Good Friday. Refuse napkins and eat beans
    like a bear.

Be ever vigilant and bold. Wander in the wilderness of God,
unmasking devils wherever they may be.

When you come upon a bad juggler, throw a stone at their hand.
Wearing a string of sausages, enter homes of the wealthy.

Know that all foolish acts rattle the cages of the comfortable
and chisel away at rules that gleam like bars, keeping the lost flock
    from grazing the kingdom.

Enter churches to wrench the pious from their piety.
Dancing up to the pulpit, pelt the priest with nuts.

Chuck a few more at the woman who refuses to open her eyes.
Close out this sermon by blowing out candles. Then run away.

All the while, care for the wretched and poor of this world. Rub
    elbows with lepers.
Do not let the boiling for your newlywed spouse drag you away

from this good path.

Once you carry out a holy deed, perform a silly act to hide
your perfection.

Some dummy who opened their mouth once said that it's a fine
line between evangelism and ventriloquism.

So shed the strings of this world. Let every movement you make
honor the Great Puppeteer.

Remember, a fool lives in flesh. So be a holy clown around your
town. Skip naked down the street. Whistle.

Only at night, set down your mask of folly and pray.

NESSIE

In 565 A.D., as Columba, the Patron Saint of Poets, Floods, and Bookbinders, prepared to cross the River Ness, he came upon men folding their dead friend into peaty earth—killed, they said, by the bite of a giant water beast. Columba was the kind of guy who drove demons out of milk pails, so when the beast rose from the waters and heathens trembled on the Scottish shore, Columba chastised the beast, telling her to "go back with all speed." She fled from his liquid voice and the Loch Ness monster never killed again. Eighteen hundred sightings later, some surmise she's a Plesiosaur, a hoax, a giant eel, a long-necked seal.

When she surfaced in '34 and got snagged in a grainy photo, looking like a witch's hat—just the crooked tip emerging—the legend unleashed, rippled murky down the Scottish Highlands through childhoods, stirring dreams, and eating sheep.

Wind blows and forty years later, the cold waters reach Kalamazoo. A girl, Patron Saint of Nothing, rescues Nessie from the newspaper and scotch tapes the monster to the inside of her closet door. Here, Nessie makes her lair. Years go by. Nessie curls and yellows, hanging on by only a brittle tooth of tape. Still up to her old tricks, she's a finger now, bent, beckoning the girl to believe. Currents shift and the girl whooshes away down the street. Nessie slips back into hiding. The nest grows old men's clothes. Push aside vines of ties and breathe in the dank. As wire bones rattle, press finger to fossilized print of tooth. Believe.

Nessie, Part Two

Since Columba predicted his own death, the world's grown crowded. We make our own monsters now, even let one loose in the Loch. It drones on, dives deep, an unblinking eye showing us how far dreams can fall. 500 feet below, to be exact.

The monsters we make show us the monsters we make, show us the 30-foot monster that sank back in 1970, a prop used to unlock *The Private Life of Sherlock Holmes*. True believers, those Patron Saints of Someday-We'll-Lay-Our-Eyes-On-Her, will not be deterred. They know, just out of sight, something wild is waiting.

THE TENDENCY OF NATURE IS FOR THINGS TO PROTRUDE, LEAVE HOME, AND WANDER

It's taken my father fifteen years to pray his way to this day.
Pressed into a Stryker bed, he studies the constellation of tiles,
counts backwards, adds up the 15 minutes it took each day to poke
the unraveling into place. All it took was a few stitches by
someone else's hand.

You're lucky, I tell him. If you had a hernia in the twelfth century,
you might have hidden away like Saint Drogo.

My father knows his saints but Drogo is news to him. He presses a
button and the head of his bed rises. *Tell me about him*, he says,
then sips water through a straw.

Orphaned at birth, Drogo's mother abandoned him for death.
After years of wandering, Drogo develops an unsightly hernia.
With intestines bulging, bearing down, he tucks his ascetic self
into a cell attached to the church of Sebourg.

The night nurse enters, takes my father's temperature and pulse.
He refuses her offer of fresh water. She leaves. *I feel foolish with
all this fussing*, he laughs. *Go on with the story.*

Years later, when the church catches fire, Drogo refuses to leave.
*If it pleases the Divine Goodness that I should escape the flames,
His will be done.* When the villagers return, they find the hermit
huddled on his knees, praying in the smoky ruins. They build him
a new womb.

Was Drogo one of those saints who never lived? my father asks,
explaining how, in the 1960s, the Catholic Church cleaned up the
calendar, yanking feast days and halos from a slew of saints.

He was the real thing, I tell him. Before he sealed himself off from the world, Drogo was a shepherd. He slept outside. Many sought his wisdom on weather and sheep.

Before I leave my father, I offer to shut the blinds.
Keep them open, he says, *I want to see the sky.*

Monica, you were bone to me

Clean and white and cold, you drummed through my elementary days, hummed below my feet as femur, other times you were a ribbed halo above my head. While I walked single-file down waxed halls, I sometimes wondered about your son, Augustine, a cathedral and school, two miles down the road. Wasn't some part of him sealed in their walls, too?

Years later, I took comfort in your rattling bones beseeching God not just for your son, but for all of us. You got things done. My self-serving tongue was less impressive. In sixth grade, it flapped this mantra: *Dear God, let me be a cheerleader*. And then, Monica Bell, three grades ahead of me, and named after you, appeared in uniform, white knee socks and saddle shoes. My mom may have called Monica's mom, but all I know is that it was a miracle. Monica in my living room, helping me learn the tryout cheer: *"Open the barn door, kick out the hay, we're for the Royals, hip, hip, hooray!"*

I imagined you much like her: patient and kind, slate eyes, and almond-colored hair spilling down a swan neck. I confess, I loved her more than you. *Make crisp, sharp movements like this,* she said, snapping her arms into and out of a broken T, like Jesus on a cross. *Let every gesture be a desire to rise up!* Even though I never made cheerleader (I couldn't quite kick out the hay) she drilled in me that movement, no matter how small, matters.

Years later, she snagged the role of Hospital Reporter #2 on *Law & Order*, season four, then moved on to Shakespeare. Around that time, all I landed was a boozy altar boy of a husband. I guess I had more in common with you, a fourth-century woman, who had married a violent pagan. The difference between us? You chose to stay and pray. I abandoned, among other things, my wedding ring. A piece of me is on Alton Street, shrouded somewhere in the mortar I mixed to wedge between yellow bricks. When it comes to repointing, mortar must be softer than its surroundings. That way, moisture escapes without destroying stone or brick. We all leave something behind. I learned that from you.

Maxine Grippo
"St. Monica" (2023)
Illustration
Courtesy of Maxine Grippo

Virginia S. Benedicte
"Saint Martin de Porres" (2022)
Image composed in collaboration with AI
Courtesy of S.D. Cason Catholic Gallery

SAINT OF THE BROOM, HELP US LEARN YOUR SWEEPING WAYS

As the patron saint of public schools,
there you are Martin de Porres,
leaning in corners, unobtrusive, humble as a broom.
You amazed with your abilities
to levitate, bilocate, and heal, but it is your holy act
of sweeping that is most impressive.

For eight long years, you swept your way through the friary,
past the novice who called you a *mulatto dog*,
past the priest who taunted you for being the illegitimate son
of a former slave and Spanish nobleman,
and right through Lima's dirty law
that forbid you from entering religious life.

Through all the snarling debris and whatever else blew in
from the streets, you made a clearing in the heart
of the Dominicans who finally ignored the law.
Then as a brother, you gathered in those brushed aside.
You tended the garden, planted orchards of olives and oranges,
lemons and figs. You kept sweeping.

Even in death, there is so much work to be done.
Take just this one math class—Lilly is hungry.
Be in the growl of her belly, fill her with grapes and grilled cheese
so she can dine on addition and add her brilliance to this world.
Bring Carlos a mentor. Help this prince of subtraction learn
he is more than the sum of a lost father and no home.

There, in the front row, is Demarcus, squinting.

Bring him glasses so he can feast on angles and light.
For those absent today—Taquavian, Mara, and Sarah—sweep
clear the darkness they tumble through: depression,
only one shoe, and younger siblings to care for.
Help them find their way back to school.

So much gnaws at us, Martin. When your fellow friars
discovered mice in the monastery chewing the altar linens,
they tasked you with poisoning them. Like you did with the mice,
whisper into the ears of our children a safe path to your garden.
Greet them each day and feed them figs among the hollyhocks,
until they are full and ripe as pears.

Whisper into our ears, too.
Bundle us together,
bristly brothers and sisters.
Let us be twined to your enduring motion.
Don't let go, Martin.
There are so many paths yet to sweep.

Israhel van Meckenem (German, c. 1445-1503)
"Saint Ursula and her Maidens"
Engraving (c. 1475/1480)
Rosenwald Collection, Courtesy of the National Gallery of Art,
Washington

DEAR URSULA OF ARCHERS, THE HUN'S ARROW NEVER FLEW

No daughter of no Christian king, at no time did you cling to your virginity and sail away from your betrothed, son of pagan king.

Not once did you board the vessel accompanied by eleven thousand maidens.

While the wind did blow for three years, it passed right through your mast that in no way sent you and your virgins down the river Rhine.

Because you never lived, poor Ursula of Archers, you did not know the end is often ugly.

Not yet the Patron Saint of School Girls, you could not stand fighting for your faith, as your companions, beheaded in no time, forever fell around you.

There, on the shore of Cologne, you couldn't comprehend the dull thud of your maidens' heads, feel them trundle across your feet.

The Hun's arrow unstrung you. Blood unbloomed, you seeped into the centuries.

ANATOMY OF PRAYER

Known for his callused and camel-like knees, James the Just, in all seasons, planted them into the sweet earth, two hardened steppingstones wearing down a path between his people and God.

My cousin wears worn knees. Jill the Cousin rarely sits around her house located—no lie—at St. James' Place. She wondered about the sainted street, took it as a sign and moved her family in.

Not one for slow-motion martyrdom, James hurled seeds of peace-filled prayers to sow justice. Before he was thrown from the top of the temple and dashed to death with stones, it's safe to bet James had been on his knees. Praying.

A living prayer, Jill's battered knees bend between God and her grown son. Down syndrome ties his tongue, keeps him from praising the one he loves who always seems to be kneeling before him—on cold bathroom tile to clean, on hard floors to collect crayons thrown across the room.

Even after he was pushed from the pinnacle, James managed to grind knees into the ground for the greater good. The knee is a hinge joint moving in two directions: toward God and others.

Not one for kneeling on street corners or standing in synagogues, Jill's scarred knees labor in secret. Even when weary, she bows down and harvests daily at St. James' Place.

Her artist daughter sees, picks up paints and creates Jill the Nurturer, her head haloed as healing bolts dancing on the palms of her lifted hands flash beyond the frame of this life. Beneath a pale blue robe, heavenly chorus of tibia and femur roll and glide.

Maxine Grippo
"Jill the Nurturer" (2020)
Painting
Courtesy of Maxine Grippo

Master H.B. (German, early 16th century)
"Saint Andrew" (c. 1530)
Pen and brown ink and gray wash
Courtesy of J. Paul Getty Museum, Los Angeles

Saint of Noticing Small Things

Andrew and his brothers drop the net; watch as it unravels tall as a tree into the Sea of Galilee. Weighed down by small stones pierced with holes and attached with care, linen roots spread out through the watery cold. In the boat, they wait. As cedar and oak sway, Andrew studies the quiet slant of hills, the familiar landscape of his brothers' hands. When the net fills, he joins the others in keeping the big fish and loosening the little ones back to sea. In between the fishing, the net demands attention: mend, wash, dry, fold. It would take a miracle for Andrew to set down this life.

*

Even away from the net he knows, Andrew notices small things. He's first to spot the boy breaking through the crowded sea of people, carrying barley bread and fish. Andrew probably calls the fish by name. *Look, that boy has five barley loaves and two musht.* Or maybe he sees that the fish are biny or sardines. Because he pays attention and speaks up, miracles happen.

*

When his friend is killed, Andrew casts himself far from the Sea of Galilee and becomes a fisher of men. He walks up and down the coast of the Black Sea. He knows what good fishermen know and sometimes wonders, *Is that enough?* He talks with anyone who will pay attention, then tells them about his friend. Mend, wash, dry, fold. *How many seas?* Mend, wash, dry, fold. *So many fish.* Black Sea salmon. Starry sturgeon. A cloud of mackerel. Then flounder, sterlet, flounder, flounder.

SAINT OF BEEKEEPERS AND BEGGARS

You were golden at birth, Ambrose,
a swarm of bees settled on your face,
leaving behind a single drop of honey.

We've heard this before, bees landing
on the breath of baby Zeus and Bacchus,
Virgil and Plato, foretelling sweetness of speech.

As sermons drip from your honeyed tongue,
we gather nectar, beat our wings ragged
to build the kingdom. Still, winter arrives,

this season of sadness in which we find
no flowers to forage. Unlike our bumbly
brothers and sisters, we do not hibernate.

In the hive of Christ, we stay awake, bodies
pressed together, shivering, generating heat
for our mother of honeycomb, candles, and bees.

Is everything we do for the queen?
The good news: we have more honey than we need.
Time now to share the sweet. Why is this so hard to do?

A NOD TO ST. NICHOLAS

Come, Nicholas, take off the black boots and red coat
you never wore. Remove pounds you never packed on
and rest now by the fire. Here, take this 'kerchief
and rub off rosy cheeks. Hand over that cherry nose
and expose your mangled one, broken when you,
Bishop of Myra, were imprisoned and tortured
all those years ago.

As light twinkles over your olive skin, help us
be like you and stand up to the emperors of today.
Do not let the blows of this world break us. Lift
the veil that keeps us hazy, snug in ourselves
and nestled under rooftops. Help us hear the unmerry
clatter of poor creatures stirring.

Like the French nuns who were inspired by you,
let us rise from warm beds and slip fruit and justice
into stockings, placing them on the doorsteps
of those who hunger. On our last good night in this world,
whether we dash away by door or chimney, may we,
like you, leave a generous trail, thick with kindness
and stirring hope.

THE POPE MUST CANONIZE A PATRON SAINT OF RATS RIGHT NOW

Oh, saints of sudden death, miscarriage of justice and babies, saints of running sores and Polish dishes, we are running out of time. We must strengthen the saints among us and canonize quickly a saint for protection from rats.

Benjamin, Lilly, Jason, even nameless girls of rural places can call upon their saints. But what about Dantrell, Tyshawn Lee, or the Jamayhas who make honor roll, go to sleepovers, and get a bullet in their back? The rats are winning and we need a saint to intercede. Hurry, their bites bleed.

Oh, Hyacinth, Saint of Weight Lifters and Pierogi, lift up this heavy prayer packed with Gertrude of Nivelles. Not to be confused with Gertrude the Great, the Gertrude we need is the Gertrude of Belgium, who had a way with field mice. In her convent she baked cakes that kept the rats away. She was a woman who knew when to let the cats out.

Join with us, Jude, Patron Saint of Hopeless Cases and pray, pray, pray, so that all that scurries may run away. Hurry, a new rat has just been born. It whisks its whiskers at 12 days old. It loses one, it grows one back. Hack off an ear, so what? Rats hear through whiskers, whiskers always growing back, whisking us to death.

Hear the king of rats scratching at the convent door? *I'll be honest. I have to tell you. I'm the very, very best healer the world has ever seen. It's a beautiful, beautiful thing. I can heal with a single steak. I'm so amazing. Listen, folks. I should be a damn saint. Hell, I'm God. Drink me. Let me in. I'm tremendous. I hate the weak, don't you?*

SINCE LIFE IS MORE THAN THIS BLUE CUP AND SAUCER

Clare of Assisi walks away from the genteel life she is expected to lead. She has her long locks cut off and welcomes the uncomfortable, her bed, the floor. She gives all her possessions away, writes, *We become what we love and who we love shapes what we become.*

She grows a convent, rubs and kisses her sisters' feet, raw and bloody from begging on the streets. *Since our bodies are not of brass and our strength is not the strength of stone*, Clare cautions them to *sacrifice seasoned with the salt of prudence …*

Did I say she grows a convent, writes her own rules? Women rules—a Middle Age miracle—rising up like little flowers, irritating the reedy skins of cardinals and popes.

One Christmas, too sick to go to Mass, and her sisters away, Clare says, *Look, Lord God, I have been left here alone with you.* Maybe because she lives a high-definition life—tuned into her God, projecting love unencrypted so others may duplicate—her Beloved blesses her, broadcasts the Mass live on her bedroom wall. They are no longer alone.

Two days before her death, Pope Innocent IV approves Clare's rules. Later, Pope Pius XII declares Clare the Patron Saint of Television.

Poor Clare, we say, when really, it's us, holed up in our palaces, our heels, soft and shiny as dinner rolls lounging on the ends of sofas. We shake our fuzzy heads—*poor Clare!*—think our reception is just fine. When mothers arrive weeping and irate uncles come to take us away, we love what is easy. Depending, we stay or we go.

Saint of the Blackbird

So as not to scare off the blackbird
that has landed on Saint Kevin's palm,
a silent thanks for bearing the delicate,
sometimes messy, nests of our making.

Saint of the Blackbird, arms outstretched
in prayer, may we learn to wait like you,
for as long as it takes our splotchy eggs
of hope to hatch and fly away.

THE UNFINISHED DANCE OF THE UNRELIABLE LEGEND, ST. VITUS

Saint Vitus' dance (also known as triste mal) became an umbrella term for an assortment of conditions with movement disorder. The association was further enhanced during the middle ages when outbreaks of dancing mania and other delirious behaviour struck Europe.

-Saint Vitus and his dance A C EFTYCHIADIS, T S N CHEN,
Journal of Neurology, Neurosurgery, &
Psychiatry 2001;70:14 doi:10.1136/jnnp.70.1.14

i.
It is 290 A.D. and Vitus is born.
As a child, he goes against his family's wishes
and becomes a Christian in a time when being one
is a crime. Not long after, his father looks through
a keyhole and sees him dancing with seven angels.
He is blinded by the vision. Vitus prays
and his father regains his sight.

ii.
303 A.D. and the stage is set.
Forty pounds of chains, a cauldron of boiling oil,
and a hungry lion. The boy, barely a teen, skirts
them all—making the sign of the cross each time—
prison turns to paradise, oil laps at his skin like tepid
bath water, the lion bows and licks his feet.

In the final scene, Vitus, along with his tutor,

and governess, is tied to a pillar and scraped
with iron claws. Cue the earthquake.
God swallows the souls of the saints.
Shrines and chapels rise up.

iii.
It is 1278. A procession of 200 singing, clapping
pilgrims dances above the Maas River. The bridge,
burdened by too many bodies, swoons and snaps.
Sweaty Christians tumble from the sky. While
most die, the injured, taken to a chapel dedicated
to St. Vitus, heal and thrive.

iv.
In 1518, Frau Troffea begins to twitch. Soon,
400 people are dancing in the Strasbourg streets.
The Dance Plague ends when exhaustion, stroke,
and heart attack cut in.

Whether seized by faith, a mental plague, or poisoned
from eating fungus-tainted rye, multitudes writhe
and howl across the centuries, a strange fusion
of palsy and prayer.

v.
It is 2016. The dance of St. Vitus begins
with limpness, brought on by rheumatic fever.
Those inflicted by the disease, drag a leg, follow
helplessly in the frenzied steps of those who sought

health and healing from a dead boy—traveled to his
statue and swayed madly before his bronzed feet.

As neurons in the basal ganglia tango, the face
grimaces and jerks. While limbs take aimless
leaps, hands milk udders of unseen cows.
As the body trembles, tongue, a flickering star,
wets the roof of night.

THE EXCLAMATION POINT NOT YET INVENTED

The monk lived in a monastery.
But it wasn't working out—the other monks considered Simeon's
ways so austere as to appear ostentatious—he was asked to leave.

Simeon dwelt in a well, later curled like a comma inside a stony
cave. Still, the world felt too wide.

One day, he stepped onto a pillar of limestone and prayed. There,
in the Syrian desert, Simeon unfurled—became the first pillar
hermit, a stark surprise to those living horizontal lives.

Atop his pillar, he stood, slept and shat for 37 years. He was a
shriek, a slammer, a bang, a startler. At dusk, even the monks
who'd cast him out could see Simeon's mark howling against the
salmon-colored sky.

People came from all over to see this pillar preacher, this
exclamation point on the end of Christian persecution. With the
path to martyrdom closed, many wondered, *How now to show love
for God?   Live boldly*, his body exclaimed from 60 feet off the
ground. *Be an emphatic declaration for God!*

When Simeon was asked by bishops and abbots to climb down, he
agreed. This monk who dictated letters from on high, signing off
Simeon the feeble had passed their test, proving himself humble in
the Lord, so his superiors told him he could stay.

When someone lives in the sky, it's only natural to want to pull
them down, to say, *Come. Come, be with us.*

Artist unknown
"Saint Simeon Stylites the younger"
Tempera painting
Courtesy of the Wellcome Collection
Public Domain

CEASELESS IS THE WORK OF SAINT AND SCIENTISTS IN RUSSIA'S LOS ALAMOS

Before he became a saint, he was Prokhor Moshnin (1754-1833), a boy born inflexibly toward God. As a monk living in Sarov, he is given the name Seraphim, derived from the Hebrew word, Seraph, meaning: to burn. And he does. Even as a hermit, Seraphim blazes for God. "Acquire a peaceful spirit," his tongue flames, "and thousands around you will be saved."

In the monastery and on the path to his hut in the forest, he stockpiles prayers of peace, bakes bread, and grows beets in his garden. Prone to being blinded by bright rays of light, the monk amasses wonders: He kindles friendships with fox and lynx. Even Misha the bear brings him gifts of leaves stuck to the hexagonal wombs of honeycombs. Seraphim feeds his wild friends from the bare, bright stars of his hands, hands he uses to claw his way up a flank of rock. There, he raises his arms, shoots off fiery rockets of praise for one thousand nights and days, eating little. He rarely winks out, but when he does, he uses a stone for pillow.

*

A hundred years later, Sarov flickers, then disappears off the map. Barbed wire winds its way around a Bethlehem that has lost its star. Shrouded in a thick cloak of fir and pine, Arzamas-16, code name for Sarov, fuses faith with human design. As scientists shepherd plutonium, the town gives birth to the Soviet's first atomic bomb. Many follow.

In 1995, Sarov slinks back onto the map, though it remains closed off. Retaining ponds pellet the landscape. Swimming is not advised. As Sarov struggles, herds of uranium wander away. On the darkest days, townsfolk and guards see an old man in a white cassock. He strikes the ground with a staff, offering a blessing perhaps, or trying to remind them what they have forgotten, that one day, while chopping wood, thieves snuck up and used Seraphim's own axe against him. Bloodied and battered, he lived, his back bent, on fire, the rest of his days.

Unknown illuminator
"The Seven Sleepers of Ephesus and their dog asleep
in a cave" (1577)
Courtesy of the New York Public Library,
http://digitalcollections.nypl.org
Public Domain

THE SEVEN SLEEPERS OF EPHESUS

In 200-plus ancient manuscripts, the story is told.
In some, the number of sleepers is three or five,
in others, unnumbered. These unnamed men
and men of many names and numbers
unfashionably believe in one God.

To avoid persecution, they flee to a cave, pray,
and promptly fall asleep. Learning their location,
the emperor orders the cave's mouth stuffed with stones.
Sealed away, they do not die but sleep four hundred
or two hundred or three hundred years. A sleeping
dog guards the cave and always the cave is dark.
If light crept in, you would see angels
turning the sleepers, back and forth.

When the stones are finally cleared away to make
use of the cave for cows, the sleepers awaken.
Feeling as if not a day has passed—and hungry—
one of them leaves to buy bread with a coin
centuries out-of-date. This draws a commotion
in the town. Perhaps there is buried treasure?
The sleepers stir the crowd by telling their story
and then slink back into one last and final sleep.

Listener! Do not get bogged down by numbers,
names, or searching for the true location of the cave.
The point is this: we all fall asleep. One emperor
replaces another. Rocked by the hands of God,
we awaken to a changed world.

Depending on the century you are in and hearing
this story, the point changes too. It's all about
resurrection. Be patient, dear listener, for rest
comes before transformation. The real point
is that God follows us to our dark caves, is always
with us. Or maybe the aim is hope. The powerful
seek to starve and wall us away, but they will not win.

No, this story shakes us awake to our own power.
Angels don't change the world. They can only
rock us as we sleep. It's our job to awaken
and rattle the world with our story,
no matter how strange it seems.

I TELL MY MOTHER ABOUT THE COMPANIONS OF THE CAVE

Ever since my father died, she's had trouble sleeping.
Because it can't hurt, I tell my mother this story.
How wonderful it must be to sleep like that,
so long and deep, she says.

Last week, my father came to her.
Dressed like an angel, in clothing
fashioned of fabrics and colors
she'd never seen before, her Joseph
hovered above the headboard.
Where did you get those clothes?

I told them you'd say that, he laughed.

Stay with me, she said and fell asleep.
When she awakened, he was gone
and she was mad at herself.
She should have reached out to hold
his hand, asked a better question,
like who was 'them'? What is it like
to sleep long and deep?

St. Genevieve, Patron Saint of Disasters, Fever, and Paris (422-512 A.D.)

It's not the devil giving us these tribulations, but the sweet boy at the gas station picking his nose and spring breakers trying to get drunk before everything closes.

We are all busy not touching our faces. Come to our aid, Genevieve. Shake off hands that reach out to touch. Protect us from sneezes, coughs, and white smiles of phony prophets. Remove from our path the person who thinks six feet is one foot. Stand with us in this time of empty stadiums. We're out of wipes. Can you get us some wipes?

Beseech God for us. Let fly your somber lips perched like red wings between two fat braids that trickle down your blue gown. And what of that bread you hold at your hips? We're all out of bread, only one pumpernickel left on the shelf. Toss us a crumb of your whole wheat faith, though sourdough will do.

Alive, you inhaled God and got by on small bits of barley bread and beans. Take us in now, lest we become host to fresh troubles. As we're hunkered at home, let us inhale you who squelched fires of fear. When Attila and his Huns crossed the Rhine, people prepared to run. You convinced them—a band of women—to remain and pray. Their eyes on God, Attila turned away.

A thousand years after your death when the burning fever trooped through towns, you cared for us. Care for us again. It's no longer possible to reach your shrine, so come unleash kindness and close distance between shuttered hearts.

Priests carried your bones down the street. People came out to touch and greet you. Even without touch, though, you saved. Favor us, Genevieve. Help us not touch. Help us save.

MY MOTHER MENTIONS IN PASSING THAT I WAS HELD BY A SAINT

After six years steeped in researching saints, I learn that in 1965, when my father called his young bride to say he was bringing his priest friend home and that he'd be staying for supper, my mother put me in the crib and yanked down *The I Hate to Cook Book* that Peg Bracken wrote "for those of us who want to fold our big dishwater hands around a dry Martini instead of a wet flounder, come the end of a long day."

She had onions, carrots, one hefty potato, beef, and a can of tomato soup, so she made Stay-abed Stew but did not dump the can of tiny peas into the casserole dish. "I never put in the peas in that dish. They don't belong," she said. "Anyways, your father was allergic to peas."

"I was ticked at your father. But at least that time he gave me a little warning after I lit into him about showing up with Charlie Heller for supper when I had only two pork chops. You were just months old and I was so tired in those days. Your father said I had postpartum depression but I kept saying, 'No, Joe. I'm just tired!' Taking care of you, cleaning, and cooking wore me out and then on top of that I was entertaining your father's priest friends. My folks always had lots of priests at our home and that is one of the reasons, I think, that your father was attracted to me."

"Father Hardon was a darling man. Brilliant. A Jesuit, you know. He was holy and humble, and he held you. That you were cradled by this saint is your claim to fame. Oh, and he was so good with you. And much nicer than the Dominican priest your father brought to the house once. That priest paid no attention to you. Oh, what was his name? I wish your father was alive. He would remember. He was a handsome priest and all the women swooned over him. He was gorgeous but demanding."

"How so?"

"I'd been cleaning, cooking, and taking care of you all day and was in the kitchen preparing supper when he shouted to me from the living room to bring him a glass of water. He didn't ask your father because he was a rude chauvinist who saw it as my job to take care of him. And when he yelled for another glass of water, I let him have it."

"Where is he now?"

"In purgatory for the way he treated women. Actually, I don't know if he's dead yet. He never came back to our house again. But he did end up leaving the priesthood to get married. Oh, his poor wife ... Come to think of it, you were held by two saints."

"Who was the other one?"

"Your father."

Master of Sir John Fastolf (French, active before about 1420 - about 1450), illuminator
"Saint Denis Holding His Head," c. 1430–1440
Tempera colors, gold leaf, and ink, Leaf: 12.1 × 9.2 cm (4 3/4 × 3 5/8 in.)
Courtesy of J. Paul Getty Museum, Los Angeles

SAINT DENIS OF MIGRAINES, BE WITH US AS WE LOSE OUR WAY

Beheaded in Paris, you continued to preach,
walking six miles before dropping your crown.
Keep us upright as we lumber blindly from bed,

walk on needles in search of medicine.
Like you, we hold our heads in our hands
as the world spins. Where is the path?

Patron Saint of Paris, you are a French ghetto now,
a mosaic of misery and chic stores. Your people
are not considered Parisian enough. In your medieval

heart they thump about, immigrants choked off.
Obstructed, they circulate amongst themselves;
oxygen grows poorer. Mosques and temples throb.

We twitch at the slightest movement.
Eyes squint, squatters steep like tea, dunked
in France's failure to welcome the stranger.

Root cellars—once lined with rampion
and rutabaga, cabbage and kohlrabi—
swell with fear and weapons.

Come, fill our cellars with pork and no pork.
Let veil and no veil rest side by side.
See us through these harsh winters.

Even as we turn away
from our neighbors,
help us yearn for light.

AN ADMIRABLE VIRGIN OF ADVANCED AGE

Apollonia stands rooted in faith, even as
stones and fists strike her face, again and again.
The Romans threaten to burn her alive unless
she bows to their heathen idols. She refuses.

Fists again, bashing her once beautiful, Egyptian face.
Teeth crackle in her mouth, remaining ones wrenched
out with pincers. This deaconess who inspired many
to convert to Christianity is offered one final chance
to cast aside her God.

She draws breath as if to speak, quieting the crowd.
With last scrap of freedom, Apollonia offers up a silent
sermon, heaving her broken body into the fire.

There is no record indicating who plucked her bones
from the ashes. Her splintered jaw is now on display
at St. Basil's, teeth lodged like sacred bullets in churches
throughout Europe. The tooth as relic, under the microscope.
This is what is gleaned of faith:

upper premolar, all angle and arch, resembles a small church.
The tooth, ripped from its once pleasing u-shaped congregation,
is covered in a cracked, white coat; edge pearled, quite rare.
Kidney-shaped surface, a gnawing prayer.

Piero della Francesca (Italian, c. 1416-1492)
"Saint Apollonia"
Painting, c. 1455-1460
Samuel H. Kress Collection, Courtesy of the National Gallery of
Art, Washington

STILL LIFE OF PARTY WITH LESSER SAINTS, MANY WHO REFUSED TO MARRY OR HAVE SEX WITH RICH, PAGAN KINGS

The wait staff, all men wearing dark suits and offering meaty appetizers, slice through the somber crowd. They pay attention and will write about each guest in years to come. The saints, satiated by fumes of faith, refuse the chicken kabobs and hot wings. A few sip water.

With wreath of blazing candles on her head, Lucy carries a silver tray with two eyeballs. Rumors roll that they are hers—the ones she gouged out or maybe the king's guard plucked them with his spear. *My name means light*, she says to anyone who will listen. Lucy averts her eyes—the new ones God miraculously plunked in her head—as Paul the Hermit, wearing only leaves, enters the room. He extends his arms and a raven flies through an open window and drops a half loaf of bread onto his weathered hand.

Juthwara of Cornwall presses two soft cheeses to her breasts to ease the ache of her father's death. This bad advice from her stepmother does not help and she, like the cheese, weeps. After the party, her stepbrother will touch her, find her garments moist. Believing the lie his mother had whispered into his ear—that Juthwara is pregnant—he will slice off her head with a sword, serving her up as the patron saint of cheese.

Soon, the music ceases. Cecilia has abandoned the organ pipes and now reclines in the corner. It was a mistake to come to the party given the axe blows to her neck three days ago. Even in death, Cecilia adds to the ambience, reposing uncorrupted, draped in silk, a mysterious and delightful smell emanating from her body. Composing, even in death.

AFTER SHOVELING NOT QUITE FIVE MINUTES

I want to give up and go inside,
instead, wonder where St. Sebaldus,
protector against cold weather, has gone.

Lost thousands of winter nights ago
in a forest of copper beech and conifer,
the hermit stumbled upon a cottage
and a poor couple invited him inside.

Their fire faint, Sebaldus told the woman
to break off icicles from their eaves.
When she returned, arms laden
with the glistening spikes, he
threw them on the wispy flames.

So many of us are lost and cold, Sebaldus.
We clear paths only to see them covered.
Bring back that night, when we blanket
strangers with welcome, our icicles
blazing like logs.

Sebald Beham (German, 1500-1550)
"Saint Sebaldus"
Engraving (1521)
Courtesy of the Wellcome Collection
Public Domain

A SOFT, UNMUSCLED GOD

A gentle-waisted Jesus,
she hangs on the cross,
two clouds of breasts
billow from her smock.
Cinched in a red bodice
smothered in gold brocade,
Wilgefortis wears a green
gown, though sometimes
it's royal blue. When it's cold,
she wears an ermine-lined cloak.

If her wrists weren't strung
with rope, she'd scratch her
beard, the one that sprouted
from stubbled prayers.
She'd hastily begged God
to make her ugly, the only
way she could think to sheer
the suitor from her side.

She hadn't fully thought it
through, that when she freed
herself—praise the Lord!—
her pagan, Portuguese King
of a father would bristle
at the sight of a bearded
daughter and crucify her.

It wasn't so bad the first
few hundred years, when

unhappy wives showered her
with prayers. Desperate
to uncumber from cruel
husbands, they grabbed
hold of Wilgefortis
with her winged hips
and implored her to fly.

Free yourself, Wilgefortis
whispers now as then, but
no one visits these days.
With one shoe off, she hangs,
debunked, bewhiskered,
gloriously broken.

SANTA LIBRADA VIRGEN Y MARTIR
Espectalissima abogada de las Señora Mugeres en sus peligrosos partos.

Artist unknown
"Saint Liberata (Uncumber, Wilgefortis)"
Colored etching
Courtesy of the Wellcome Collection
Public Domain

RESURRECTION HERE, AMONG THE TOMBS

Step down and enter this wildly forgotten and open
place dug into earth's bowels, diggers long dead, a scene
of temporary burials where life emerges from decay;
just ask the one who sways your way—the regal peacock.
In this underground offering, graffiti and prayers feather
catacomb walls where benches once lined up like trains,

waiting for families to picnic with their dead. A train
of ridiculously long feathers sweeps the dark, an open
invitation from this groom garbed in watchful feathers
as he dances for his dull bride who's fled the scene.
Vehicle of forgotten gods and guests, the peacock

cries, then flies away, lamps quiver amidst decay.

Even though each century deposits its own decay,
Christ mixes into the mud of history. Hands train
to take away the hardened womb of days: peacock,
dove, and lamb restored, visible once more. Open
the catacombs, a tangle of tombs rarely seen,
here, martyrs' bones stirred by feathers.

But then, the bird shrugs off its finery of tail feathers;
beauty scatters. As another season incites decay
plumage of darkness spreads and obscures the scene.
Do not run away. Wait for splendor to arrive. Train

yourself to stay, just be. When the dazzling returns, open
your eyes. Don't be afraid to touch the shimmering peacock

perched above the stable. Head in the stars, the peacock
reflects the light with its new cascading coat of feathers.
He cries out, awakens the graves of thieves and saints, open
now to mystery, to flesh that lives and won't ever decay.
No need for tickets, just board the everything-is-possible train.
First stop: a beardless, baby God at the nativity scene.

Flannery O'Conner once wrote a scene
in which there entered a stunning peacock—
tail "flowed out on either side like a floating train"
and then upon witnessing the spread of feathers
her priest declared, "Christ will come like that!" Decay
shall be no more, the extravagance of God open
to all who take in the final scene, showered in feathers.
Behold, the peacock's flesh does not decay.
Heed the call to ride this wild train; for you, the door is open.

Garrylee McCormick
"The Savior"
Icon Painting
Courtesy of Garrylee McCormick

SEARCHING

Her nose drips
green pepper,
small mounds of moist
meat round out chin and cheeks.
Mary on meatloaf.

Her son is turning up in odd locations—
on a clean, crumpled sock in England.
In the States, he's seared himself into a stick of fish,
burnt his profile into a wedge of Texas toast.
Somewhere else, her snack-sized son is a Cheeto
curled in prayer.

She wants to lean on Joseph, tell him
this is no way to save the world
but her husband is nowhere to be found.
So Mary gathers up her congealed veil of holy
and seeps into the whorled, wooden door of the
Riddle family trailer.

She is closing in on her boy,
every grain of her being ablaze.

Garrylee McCormick
"Holy Mother of God"
Icon Painting
Courtesy of Garrylee McCormick

PATRON SAINT OF DIFFICULT MARRIAGES

Not to be confused with chalice, cilice squelches the thirst of flesh. It's a shirt made from the rough hair of goat, like the one St. Hedwig of Silesia bears under her clothes after she's borne seven children.

Before a bishop, she and her husband, First Duke of Silesia, vow a life of continence. Henry refuses purple and never shaves again. Beneath grey, Hedwig wears a belt with sharp points, turned inwards. Each prick enters her body, a beam of clean light.

While her husband weds himself to work, claiming conquests of Krakow and castles not yet crumbled, she seeks comfort in discomfort, her body itching, itching, always itching. Between them, they help each other to heaven, building churches, hospitals, and convents.

When Hedwig meets up with Henry the Bearded, it is only in public places—at festivals, openings of churches, and over the graves of their children. In a fallen state, they stand as one flesh, and refrain from touch. Sometimes, the smell of earth is almost more than Hedwig can bear. She'll thrust her face into the dirty wash water of nuns and refuse to scratch.

Unknown illuminator
"Saint Hedwig Washing the Feet of Lepers;
The Burial of Saint Hedwig's Husband Heinrich," 1353
Tempera colors, colored washes, and ink, Leaf: 34.1 × 24.8 cm (13
7/16 × 9 3/4 in.)
Courtesy of J. Paul Getty Museum, Los Angeles

DAILY MORTIFICATION, PRESCRIPTION FOR THE SOUL

Even a sot who steals a man's fiddle can become a saint, like Matt Talbot, the Dublin drunk, one of 12 children, who at the age of 12 took to drink. At 28, he raised himself from the dead of drunk, his first miracle of sorts, followed by a daily chain of miracles stretching 40 sobering years until, when on his way to Mass, he dropped dead on Granby Lane. His life would have gone unnoticed were it not for the heavy chains and metal cords discovered swaddling his body.

You, too, can subdue the mortal appetites that weigh us down. No need to flog the flesh with stinging nettles. No sackcloth required. Forego spiked chains worn around thighs until the dinner hour. To unbind yourself from body simply place pebbles in your shoes. Walk a distance. Then stop. Stand on the tips of your toes. Fixing your gaze on God, pirouette. Spin away. Enshrine this whirlish moment, for each swirl unshackles a soul. Remember, heaven's door turns on your pain.

Saint Gemma Galgani, Daughter of Passion (1878-1903)

After Michael Dunn's "Accidental Markings, No. 153"

Every Thursday I begin to die. It is the best part of my week. Oh, to take leave of this miserable flesh! My trembling lips refuse the soup and I excuse myself from the supper table and go to my room. Removing my scratchy wool cloak, hair shirt, and knotted cording with nails girding my waist, I could almost laugh—how these poor instruments of penance make but a shabby dint on my soul.

Wound me, Jesus. Let me lighten your burden and take on your suffering. To grow, we need hard bread, yes? Give me your crusted hand. Let me kiss your beautiful brow scourged from your crown of thorns. My earthly pain is nothing compared to yours.

As my body transforms—sweet relief!—shame spills away. Into the pillow seeps the house servant who took me into a closet and undressed me. Anger inside me drains. Bless the woman who refused me entry into the convent—if only I could be a nun!—and praise the priest to whom I confess my sins; he ignores my letters as if I am nothing.

My aunt pushes open the door to my room. Nail marks the size of a penny shine in the middle of my palms and on my feet. Blood flows from scratches on my forehead. Here, for you, my body as sermon. As my breasts heave, witness my woman-Christ body bleed. No man priest needed to feed me my Lord. Jesus with his enormous heart has entered me. The cage of my chest is too small to contain his love. Three of my ribs bend to hold Him. We thunder as one, drunk with pain.

No one sees the sewing needle on the floor. They are too busy following priestly orders, scribbling down all my body has to say. Note this: In winter, Jesus hardly looks at me. The agony is more than I can bear. I fling my wretched self, headfirst, down a well. My hair roots in darkness for my Love. Why has He abandoned me? Just as I am about to shatter, an invisible hand pulls me out. The path to Him is brutal.

Michael Dunn
"Accidental Markings, No. 153"
Ink Drawing
Courtesy of Michael Dunn

UNDERWATER JESUS

It takes work to find him. Weather permitting, go to the shoreline
of Little Traverse Bay. Line up with hundreds of others and trek
across the frozen water. Wait your turn. Strain to hear someone
two behind you brag about this being their third time. Hear
someone else say, *the deeper the wreck, the slower the decay.*
When it's time, kneel over the ice hole. Say a small prayer
for chainsaws with teeth that bite through four feet of ice,
the depth of a small nephew. Peer into the viewing box
and down through 21 feet of water. Do not hide your
disappointment. You'd hoped for a green God, one
adorned with mossy thorns. Instead, divers have
scrubbed this one clean, removed the marine
crust that would have made him interesting.
Time's up. Leave him, sleeping in the water,
eyes closed.

HAVING BOUGHT ST. JOSEPH, I BURY HIM

Hundreds of years ago, when nuns needed more land to build convents, they buried St. Joseph medals and prayed to this patron saint of family and household needs. Today, thousands of home sellers and real estate agents have adopted this practice, burying a statuette upside down on the property of the home. The St. Joseph Statue, "Your Underground Real Estate Agent Kit" has everything you need to successfully bury your own St. Joseph Statue. Be it fact or be it fiction, it's worked more than once.

   St-JosephStatue.com

My unchurched friend
tells me it is well past time,
so, unaided, as rain

mixed with pine and
thick as molasses seeps
into my bent back,

I pry open the earth
with a trowel, dig a
simple grave—

a watchful place
from which he will
mind the white house

with black shutters.
I press his plastic body
cloaked in a peach robe

headfirst,
into the swollen
ground;

place a pinecone
atop his
hollow feet,

then run to the car
my body drawing
back drapes

of rain.
In my haste
I will forget

the most
important part
of the burial instructions:
You must pray to him,
this earthly father,
to intercede on your behalf.

Later, I will tell
my friend that because
I was infused in faith—

which wasn't orderly
at all but soiled
and sticky with resin—

I didn't bother
to clean my hands, just
let them speak

for themselves,
seize the wheel
and drive away.

Garrylee McCormick
"St. Joseph"
Icon Painting
Courtesy of Garrylee McCormick

YOU MIGHT BE A SAINT

if from cradle onward, you show no mark
of levity. Born of a mother who offers
little milk from swollen breasts, you suckle
mere seconds, suffice on drops that satisfy
not even a mouse.

Drawn to weeping ulcers of lepers' feet,
you prefer to eat not with a spoon
but a stick, a stick you press into the dirt
floor and drag along as hunger paces
in its cage of flesh.

Desire rises on hind legs and roars.
Your body is a lion you back into the corner.
You won't let it rest, try to tame it with twigs
and rusty wires that wound. As it crouches,
crack the whip.

Drag the stick until it kisses a beetle's back.
Peck hard. Even as the gangrenous sore
swells the arm—will one day spread to wrist,
to hand to fingertips—you manage to bring
the broken to your lips.

Eat the twitching, tell yourself you are satisfied.

BACK WHEN I WAS A SEVEN-YEAR-OLD SAINT

Draping a white towel over my head,
I'd pretend to be an Albanian nun.
Did Mother Teresa have this much fun?

I could feel the Son next to me
as we leaned over the bathroom sink
and cared for my beautiful leper

Baby Tender Love. As crippled Ken
and blind Barbie waited their turn,
I tried to *do small things with great love.*

I'd wash my leper's hair with Breck,
banish crayon marks from her skin,
then soothe her with song.

Everything seemed so simple then,
black and white like the bathroom
tile my mother scrubbed each week

even as Vietnam invaded our living room
through the Zenith television because
we've forgotten we belong to one another.

Finding it hard to stay holy,
I'd transform into Cher,
swinging my terrycloth hair,

Sonny with me as we bellowed
into Mr. Potato Head's deaf ears,

I've got you, babe.

UNPACKING THE HAZELNUT

Oh, holy hermit, by anchoring yourself to the church of St Julian
in Norwich and allowing yourself to be sealed up in that small cell,
you remind us that, we too, are walled up in bodies that eventually
fail us. Some of us have already succumbed.

Even as waves of Black Plague swept thousands of your
townspeople away, you held on. Despite our fears, keep open for
us at least one small window to this world so that, like you, we can
greet the street pilgrims passing by.

God once showed you a little thing, slipping a hazelnut into the
palm of your hand. In darkness and blazing with fever, you
glimpsed God in this small brown globe, saw the sum of the entire
world.

Like hazelnuts, we abide in skins of hard helmets, holding the
sweet inside. *Everything to know of God is here.* With so much in
this life waiting to be seen, may we be brave enough to drop from
branches we cling to and crack wide open.

In casting off the hard husks keeping us from each other, let us
join with deer, ruffed grouse, and quail, and feast on the sweet all
around us.

Patron Saint of the Selfish, Who Once Wore the Most Exquisite Clothes

For those who won't give up time or money,
who queen over others and refuse to share,
Jeanne de la Noue is the saint for you.
If you're tempted to take the biggest piece of cake
or the last slice of health care, there is hope.

Only six when her father died, she worked in her family's
store, selling draperies, rosaries, and holy trinkets to those
making their way to Notre Dame des Ardilliers.
Considered bossy, coquettish, selfish, and small,
Jeanne reigned over the house and the shop.

When her mother died, Jeanne's hunger for wealth grew.
She opened the shop on Sundays and Holy Days and her pockets
swelled. In 1698, an old widow visited her store, in which
no beggar could hope to find a crust at her door. War and famine
visited too but it was the woman she turned away who changed
            her,
told her she is meant for more than making money.

To close up shop on selfishness, start small.
Begin by giving away your best dress.
Take in an orphan and sleep in a hard chair.
Turn your house into a home for others. When it fills, let
            prostitutes

and the forgotten spill into your caves along the River Loire.
Give the poor your warmest blankets and tuck them in at night.

Friends and family may question your motives, say you're not
sincere.
The righteous will pronounce your faith too fervent.
Continue to rise early for others. You might even sleep in a shroud
so dirty you too might be called *the Pig of Jesus Christ*.
You won't have time to consider if this is an insult or an honor.
You won't care; you'll be too busy wallowing in the Christ of
others.

TAKE UP THY SNOWBALL

Born near the mouth of the Meuse, Lidwina skates steadily through the Netherlands.

At 14, just a spit of a girl, she slips on ice and breaks a rib. Things begin to snowball, as in her inward bruise tumbles down, gets faster and faster, bigger and bigger, absorbing everything in its path. Her brother William gets left behind as the world forms around Lidwina. Her parents trail after her crumbly mess, pick up bits of her bone and skin that drop off—and place them in a vase.

Things continue to go downhill. Life compacts until Lidwina, save for head and left hand, is unable to move.

Her family rolls her onto a bed of straw. She uses a stick, whittled from cypress, to open and close the curtains. She prays, eats smidgens of cinnamon and sugar and has visions. Sometimes, she sips watered wine.

Just to breathe, Lidwina sometimes leaves her body buried in all that snow—returns with the most fantastic tales—how she followed angels to churches, ran through meadows, and rambled throughout Rome.

One night, William leaves watch of her, but not before placing a burning candle out of reach. The candle tips over. As flames lick her straw bed, she fears melting and begins to pray. Her left hand snuffs out the fire.

"Lidwina's fall on the ice"
Wood drawing from John Brugman's *Vita of Lidwina* (1498 edition)
Public domain

THE INEFFABLE SWEETNESS OF HER MILKY GLORY

Catherine's taken by the bedridden
young woman, her frozen limbs, the scantiness
of her nourishment, the glorious mystery
of her pains and silent suffering.

As Catherine runs a cool cloth over her
charge's chest, she lingers over stiff nipples,
tells Lidwina she's had a vision: come
Christmas, Lidwina's breasts will swell
with milk. Catherine is to taste of this milk.
When Lidwina lifts her left hand in protest—
the only part of her body she can still move—
her caregiver chides her, tells her not to doubt.

Christmas night arrives. As Lidwina lies motionless,
a multitude of maidens suddenly appears. Naked,
they encircle her, shimmering stars of dew.
Mary is with them, her belly in full bloom.
Lidwina watches as Mary squats, cups her hands
to her swollen sex and brings forth the babe.
Milk flows, soft mounds of maidens' bosoms grow.

Lidwina, thrilled by the heaviness, the deep ache,
is surprised to find the fingers of her left hand
pursuing her own small mounds.
Catherine enters the room, sinks to her knees,
and leans over Lidwina. She smells sweetness.
Hungry, her mouth suckles one nipple, then the next.
Lidwina feels her skin melting; her heart,
a dark egg, quivering in a nest of straw.

CUNIGUNDA, THE SLAPPING SAINT

Waiting for the movie to start my soon-to-be-divorced friend leans over the popcorn and says, *Saint Cunigunda. You know her? No,* I whisper. Later, I'll look her up.

She married Saint Henry the Exuberant, who wasn't yet exuberant nor a saint. When they wed, he was just the Duke of Bavaria, later crowned king of Germany, and she became queen. In lieu of children, they raised churches, showered money on monasteries, and cared for the poor.

Because they had no children, stories rose up that theirs was a chaste marriage. As the Devil could not tempt the couple, he donned the body of a knight and for three mornings in a row exited her bedroom, stirring rumors among the king's court. To prove herself innocent, Cunigunda walked barefoot over searing plowshares. Her unscathed feet proved her fidelity.

One time, with a candle still lit, she and her maid fell asleep in her chambers. They awakened to the bed burning. Cunigunda made the sign of the cross and the fire went out. Another time, she slapped the cheek of her frivolous niece for not keeping holy the sabbath. The mark where she lay her hand never disappeared.

I see why my friend is drawn to this slapping saint. While she doesn't have a frivolous niece, her husband comes close. He's busy buying roses and arranging candlelit dinners for a lover he denies is his lover, even though he splatters Facebook with these escapades and changes his status to "engaged." My friend is tired of being a miracle maker, preparing the house for market, caring for their kids, and doing astonishing works at her job. She wants to let down her wings, go on the Jerry Springer Show, and fling chairs. Like Saint Cunigunda, she wants to prove herself worthy, wants to burn without being consumed, and leave her mark.

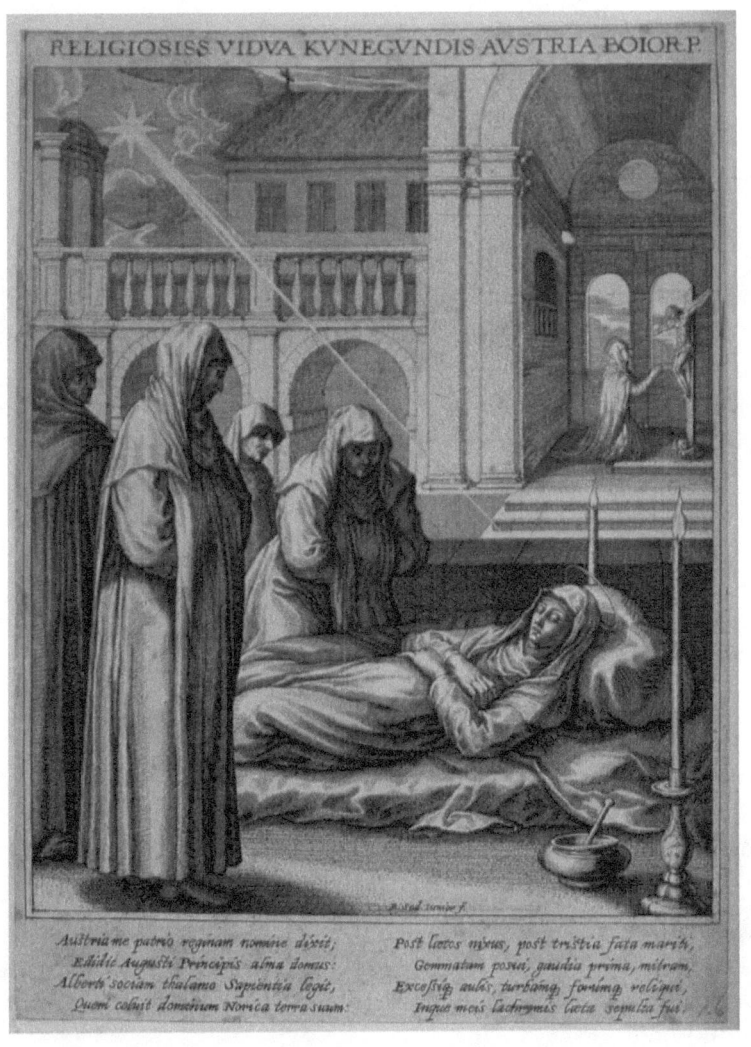

Raphael Sadeler II (Flemish, 1584-1632)
"Saint Cunegund"
Line engraving
Courtesy of the Wellcome Collection
Public domain

THE SAD AND DISTURBING STORY OF ELEVEN-YEAR-OLD MARIA GORETTI (1890-1902)

How it begins

The telling almost always begins on her last day, a hot July, her father dead, her poor mother and brothers threshing in fields they don't own, as Maria sits on the steps, sewing Alessandro's shirt, though sometimes she is in the kitchen they shared with him and his drunk of a father. As she sews or cooks for the families and cares for her younger siblings, 20-year-old Alessandro slips away from the field and touches her. He burns for her. She refuses him.

Back up. Why doesn't the story start months earlier, when she is a drop in an ocean of fear, Alessandro circling like a shark? He cuts her with crude comments, whispers through white teeth that he'll kill her if she tells. As he circles and circles, Maria thinks, why heap worry on her mother's grief?

If this were a movie, it would begin with curtains drawn, as we eat popcorn and watch him strike her with an awl, eleven times in the front and three more in the back as she tries to run for help.

Left up to me, I'd start with a slipper flying through the air, Maria ducking, moments after she's begged her mother not to be left alone with him. But other than throw a shoe, what else is a widow with six children to do?

It rarely starts here, at the core of the story, under blinding lights and surrounded by surgeons, Maria stunning them all before she dies. *May God forgive him, because I have already forgiven him.*

Appearing in dreams

After death, she gets busy. To her brother Angelo she says, *Go to America—there's money there.* He goes and finds money.

To another brother fighting the Germans, she warns him to stay in the trenches. As his companions charge with bayonets, he alone survives.

She finds her killer in prison, hands him fourteen white lilies, one for every gouge he gave her.

When her killer is released from jail, he visits Maria's mother and asks her forgiveness. Like Maria, she forgives him,

but unlike her daughter, she will not be made a saint. She is no virgin.
And after her death, she'll refuse to visit him in her dreams.

The problem with this story, and others

Virginity is cast a starring role. Notoriously difficult to work with, Virginity, a textbook narcissist, refuses to come out of her trailer. She won't work with other female cast members unless she's the center of attention. Without her, Virginity believes, they would all be spoiled. She is their savior. And though she's not a team player, she's cast again and again because someone keeps writing tiresome, unhelpful stage directions: *Virginity remains. Better the rest of the cast be killed, rather than broken and bruised, and left alive without her.*

Perfect fruit, Pope Pius XII called Maria. Her killer, already ripened to this notion, agreed. *Maria was right to let herself be killed,* he said, felt lucky for attempting to pluck a saint—*my little saint*—he'd refer to Maria, as if he owned her, made her.

95

If the script ever flips and calls for this no-talent nothing Virginity to play Maria, she will not hold up. Let's start the story here. On the cold table, under bright lights, Virginity, unable to utter Maria's lines, simply disappears.

THE HOLY PREPUCE

halo to the penis, foreskin of baby Jesus
rising into the heavens

crowning the Jewel of the Solar System
ring of flesh transformed into rings of Saturn

coming back down to earth
making incredible rounds—

a present regifted by Charlemagne
reposing in the hands of Pope Leo III

tumbling on the tongue of Agnes Blannekin
slick as the skin of an egg

(she confesses to swallowing
the greatest sweetness again and again)

slipping onto the finger of Catherine of Siena
a soft wedding ring

on display in eighteen churches at once
then making way to an Italian village

and even though ten Pope Leos later,
the very mention of the membrane

is banned, it's dragged from a shoebox
in the closet of a priest, and as part

of the circumcision feast, paraded each year
before believers swelling the streets

until 1983, the relic, resembling a red
chickpea, disappears without trace.

WHEN MY MOTHER CALLS, I TELL HER I'M RESEARCHING THE HOLY PREPUCE

So odd, that feast day, she says. We used to celebrate it on January first. I'm glad the Church has replaced it with the Feast of the Holy Family. That reminds me—have I ever told you this?—of when I was teaching at the university, pregnant with your brother. I had the most peculiar colleague. He'd lock himself in his office and write poems mourning the loss of his foreskin. He refused to answer his students' knocks, so they always trailed like lost ducks down to my office. *How did you know what he was writing?* I asked. His wife told me. She worried about him. He just couldn't stop quacking about his lost foreskin. You should write about something else. Do you miss your tonsils?

SAINT THECLA AND THE MONK SEALS

Back in 40 A.D., when marriage was a moral responsibility, for three days and nights, I latched like a spider's web to my window. Listening to Paul preach on the roof next door unraveled something inside me. How my mother despised this man for disrupting our noble lives. She called on my betrothed, Thamyris. *Ugly, foreigner, bowlegged, bald*, they called Paul. But no matter, I could not be moved.

Despite their pleas, I gave myself permission to untether and traveled through Turkey preaching like Paul. Unleashing myself like that scared my mother. She tried to pin me down, demanded I be tied naked to a stake and burned alive. After the heavens opened and foiled the flames, I managed to get away.

It wasn't long after, I got sentenced to death again, this time tossed into an arena with lions and bears. Jumping into a watery pit swarming with seals, I baptized myself. Before the creatures could devour me, God threw down lightning and pierced their bodies. I went on teaching and preaching.

Thinking back on those seals, they must have been Mediterranean Monk ones, endangered now, 700 at most. Harassed like me who, though I learned to travel unaccosted along Roman roads, dressed as a man. The seals too, learned to change their ways. Until the 18th century, they lounged and gave birth on open beaches. They now seek caves along ragged coastlines, their pups often drowning or dashed against the rocks.

I lived out my days in a mountain cave. After learning Thamyris had died, I returned home briefly as I missed my mother. All those years, she had carried the net I dropped at her feet, its emptiness of grandchildren weighing her down. Refusing to cast it aside, she pretended to be a stone so nothing I said could reach her. I finally left, weeping.

In my cave, I prayed and healed those who sought me out. Women named their girls after me, engraved my name on their oil lamps and my face on their tombs. Even long after I'd died, people made pilgrimages to shrines built in my name and listened as the *Acts of Thecla* were read aloud.

Today I fade away in a cave near the Aegean Sea where someone in the sixth century painted me standing next to—and equal to—Paul, though someone has come along and blinded my eyes and scratched the raised fingers of my right hand. As if that could take away a woman's power.

Just like my mother, others through the centuries have tried to tame me. In 1969, the Church I helped to make snatched away my halo and claimed I was nothing more than pious fiction.

No one talks of me anymore. But I won't be silenced for long. The seals, once on the verge of extinction, hold on.

"Saint Thecla"
Fresco (11th century) in Saviour Cathedral of Chernihiv, Ukraine
Public domain

RELICS OF THE FLESH

In 1583, a year after St. Teresa of Avila's death,
Father Gracian leans into the casket and severs
her left hand as well as the pinky from her
right hand, the one that once wrote: *Christ has no body
now but yours. No hands, no feet on earth but yours.*

He sends the hand to her Carmelite convent in Avila,
keeps the little finger for himself, wears it around
his neck.

He weeps and writes: *She loved me, and I her,
more tenderly than any other creature on earth.*
He orders one seat remain vacant in every Carmelite choir.

Two years later, he opens the casket again, gazes at her
uncorrupted body, the moles on her face, hairs in them,
standing like soldiers. He cuts off her left arm.

*

Everyone wants a piece of this *unworthy Servant.*
Someone snatches Teresa's heart, right hand.
There goes the faithful partner of her left foot,
with her every step of the way as she founded
monasteries and convents throughout Spain.

Her jawbone is stolen. It danced when she said,
May God protect me from these gloomy saints.

An unnamed priest kisses her arm
and when nuns aren't looking, nibbles off
a bit of skin and squirrels it away in his cheeks.

Her four-hundred-year-old arm brings comfort to General Franco.
He takes it with him wherever he travels, leaving his wife behind.

*

Her saintly parts restore sense of smell,
heal maladies of the throat and eye.
Behold, soil from her grave cures gout.
Even splinters from her coffin work miracles.

THREE BLACK POPES

Three Black popes. See how they vanish.
They walked into the Church one day, but
their African features got brushed away.
Three white popes. Three white popes.

When Victor walked through the doors in 189,
Easter was celebrated on different days.
So this African sage who once said *I did not bear
my gray hairs in vain* got Christians on the same page.
Pope Victor the First.

In 311, when Miltiades stepped into the Church,
the flock was in disarray, the previous two popes
having been driven away. A true shepherd of peace,
he convinced emperors to loosen their chains and gathered
the scattered and lost. Pope Miltiades.

Gelasius came along in 492 and required church riches
to flow through the door to support the struggling,
the weak, and the poor. A most prolific pope,
he wrote hymns and letters and then wrote
some more. Pope Gelasius the First, the last

Black pope. Despite artists renderings
that wiped history away, truth can be restored
when we say their names: Victor, Miltiades,
and Gelasius. Three. Black. Popes.

Virginia S. Benedicte
"Three African Popes" (2022)
Image composed in collaboration with AI
Courtesy of S.D. Cason Catholic Gallery

NUMBERED OUR DAYS: MAXIMILIAN KOLBE

It is 1941. The 49-year-old Polish priest
who hid more than 2,000 Jews in his friary
is one of more than 15,000 Poles registered
as a political prisoner in Auschwitz.

Outside Barracks 14, bones with skin
stand at attention, punishment for a man
gone missing. Through the cold night,
they crowd together like bees and wait
for morning's sting.

They line up for roll call and ten men
are picked to die. When one pleads
for his life, what of his two sons? his wife?
Prisoner #16670 steps out of line and says,
I will go instead of this man.
5659 can only thank 16670 with his eyes.

When 16670 was a child, Mother Mary
came to him offering one of two crowns.
To take the white crown meant he would
persevere in purity. Red, he'd be a martyr.
He took both. When he grew up, he said,
I see Mary everywhere.
I see difficulties nowhere.

Herded to Block 11, cell #18, the men
are forced to strip, left to starve. Nothing
adds up in the 8 X 8 hunger bunker.
Sun slips its shiny fingers around

the bars of the basement window.

Zero screams or begging this time. Guards
and prisoners alike surprised by the drone
of hymns and prayers. The prisoner who
took the place of a stranger leads the men
in prayer.

One by one the men die. 14 days later,
with three still alive, a man with a name
steps inside and injects carbolic acid
into their left arms. 16670, who once
said, *The most deadly poison of our times
is indifference,* is last to die.

Life becomes more harshly concentrated
for 5659 as fellow inmates blame him
for killing their priest. After surviving
5 years, 5 months, and 9 days, 5659
reunites with his wife. She tells him
their two sons did not survive the war.
He sees his dead sons everywhere.

In 1982, Pope John Paul II declares Maximilian Kolbe
the Patron Saint of our Difficult Century.
Nobody declares 5659 anything though
he spends the rest of his days telling people
about the man who saved him.
53 years after his life was spared,
he dies at 93. His second wife says,
Now, he has gone to Kolbe.

Unknown photographer
"Maximillian Kolbe" (1894–1941)
Photograph (1936)
Public Domain

THE CARDINAL HAS FLOWN AWAY

Jerome kneels on hard earth, beating his breast with a stone. The cardinal has flown away and in this moment he is his true self, a ragged sparrow perched on the mountaintop, banging wing to chest—his feeble attempt to take flight from sin.

Between each knock rattling heaven's gate, memories of his old bones young assail him. Heat, scorpions, and wild beasts fade away and the dancing girls rush in. Ah, the pleasures of Rome! Everything hurts these days so how is it he's bewildered by desire? Wearied, too, by virgins who fall daily and troops of eunuchs who fail to heed his words. He denies himself fruit and warm water.

Jerome is blind to the lion lounging under the leathery leaves of the olive tree and has no memory of the lion limping into the monastery, or of grasping the golden tweezers as the other monks gasped, so close to terror's hot breath as he plucked the thorn from the giant paw.

This moment that never was—defines him, and the lion follows him everywhere. So much to tame in this world. So many thorns yet to pluck. The wild is calling. Soon the candle will quiver out.

Joos van Cleve (Flemish, circa 1485-circa 1540)
St. Jerome in Penitence
Oil on wood panel, circa 1516-18
Collection of the Muskegon Museum of Art, Hackley Picture Fund
Purchase, 1940.47

To all the B saints

You pay attention to the barbers and bankers, look out for the boy scouts—ready or not here they come to merit the day and oh, yes, let us not forget the builders, the bi-racial, the betrothed.

To you B saints looking out for the blind and the broken, and to all those bending in times of trouble for bowels and breasts, directly beseeching on behalf of brides and even that bachelor wearing a boutonniere of bruises.

A toast to the brewers, a pat to the bakers, flicking Bics to the candlestick makers falling in with the C saints, the alphabet of holy marching on.

ADDRESSING THE FLAXEN SPIRIT, NOT YET LINEN

Threshing

We come from deep loam,
from fields of green, blue heads bobbing.
To harvest true selves and loosen seeds within,
permit wind to winnow away the clutter.

Retting

To release fiber from stem,
baptize in slow-moving waters,
or even dew.

Do not over-ret, for, as with anything,
there is danger of growing weak,
and breaking.

After the retting

the scutching begins.
Baptism is never enough.
To transform woody selves
to strands of silky smooth,

press against the sharp edge
of life. Prepare to spin

with the moaning
earth.

Heckling

is the hardest part,
but it must be done—
we must separate
from our selves
to be spun into one.
Be still and comb
the heart, untangle
worry, part from grudges,
brush away the last stray
residues of this hardened
life we cling to.

Nothing to weigh us down,
readied now,
to be woven.

JOB POSTING

TITLE: SAINT

OBJECTIVE: Looking for a customer-oriented, deceased individual to act as a liaison between Heaven and Earth, provide information to God and resolve, with celestial speed and accuracy, any and all problems shared by the wretched in their time of need. This enlightened individual will inspire faithful customers while generating new leads and developing accounts worldwide.

RESPONSIBILITIES:
— Storm heaven, rattle and whisper into the ear of God.
— Prepare all outgoing correspondence, no matter how raggedy it may be, such that the Big Guy in the sky will pay attention.
— As part of a cloud of witnesses, rain down. Fill our empty pails, pails we've placed on stoops, in hopes they don't get kicked aside and forgotten.
— Be with us in times of trouble.
— Be with us in times of despair.
— Be with us.

QUALIFICATIONS:
-The ideal candidate is a "go-getter," willing to work on behalf of anyone who calls upon them, be they housewives, painters, thieves, or jugglers, and go get their prayers answered.
-Familiarity with pain and suffering. Experience being burned at a stake or beheaded a plus.
-Must be regarded as holy/reputation for holiness. Can't be just a moment of feeling holy, like that time, on your knees, you wept with your mother as you scrubbed the bathroom floor.
-Except in the case of martyrs, show proof of miracles. (We're confident martyrs go directly to heaven, but those dying a natural death are another matter.) Minimum of two miracles required and

must be performed *after* death. Please note that over the centuries we have tightened our requirements so incorruptible body no longer suffices as miracle. In an attempt to free the body from chains of decay, too many of the living have been caught basting bodies in chemicals, tucking herbs under skin.

-Miracles that don't count: Finding that great parking space near Talbots when the outlet mall was packed. Escaping a bad marriage.

-Candidate must live in Heaven. Miracles serve as proof of residence, letting us know you are in Heaven and in good standing. Otherwise, what would be the point?

-Must command persuasive powers. Why should God listen to the cries of a murderer, contrite though he may be?

-Requires strong follow-through skills. Prior to your death, if you say something mysterious like, *I will let fall a shower of roses from heaven,* follow this up! Emit the smell of roses from your corpse. Appear as a rose in unexpected places.

-Which reminds us, Odor of Sanctity is a plus. Walking on water—plus, plus. Raising somebody from the dead—plus, plus, plus.

-Show patience; recognize that those on earth get easily confused and may pray *to* and not *with* you. In those instances, petitions may be ignored.

-Must be willing to travel at all hours of the day and night.

-Must feel comfortable being in four or fifty places at once. (Our saints find that the more successful they are, the more often they are called upon for assistance.) Be prepared to go to dank basements, bedrooms, cubicles, and into pickup trucks barreling down the highway.

COMPENSATION:

This is an outstanding opportunity to assume a pivotal role in the fast-paced world of disease, flood, famine, terrorism, and environmental degradation. While the position does not include a salary, 401(k) plan, or vacation benefits, we are prepared to offer a compensation package. We may enshrine your left toe or right thigh. Your torso may be mounted; your head passed around like a cold potato. Masses will be offered in your honor and Feast Days held in your memory. Churches and children will be named after you.

ADDITIONAL CONSIDERATIONS:
While many feel called to this work, few will be venerated. Currently, an estimated 10,802 saints are somewhere out there supporting millions. The world needs more. St. Jude, Patron Saint of the Impossible, is entirely too busy these days and can only be in seventy-two places at one time. We are currently in negotiations with Patron Saints of Shoemakers, Blacksmiths, and others, who, for thousands of years, have faithfully looked over professions that have dwindled or gone by the wayside. With time on their rotten hands and hands that have been stolen, lost, and encased in glass, our hope is that these saints will convert to handle First World problems (i.e., remote control is misplaced and favorite show is about to start, pizza box doesn't fit in the fridge). If we succeed in these talks, you can anticipate a reduced workload.

The above is intended to describe only the most basic requirements for the performance of this job. It should not be construed as an exhaustive statement of duties and responsibilities. Qualified and interested candidates should refer to canon law. Submit nothing for consideration.

NOTES

When I told my mother I was pulling together some notes for this book, she asked, "Do people *have* to read these notes?" I'll tell you the same thing I told her. No, you don't *have* to read them. But I hope you do.

"Linen women, with a nod to St. Catherine of Alexandria, Patron Saint of Seamstresses" and "Addressing the flaxen spirit, not yet linen"

Like many martyrs of her day, this Egyptian-born saint met a gruesome end because of her unwavering faith. Then Roman Emperor Maxentius, irritated that **Saint Catherine of Alexandria** (287-305) was converting so many Roman citizens to Christianity, convened 50 pagan scholars and philosophers to debate her. She debated brilliantly and won them all over to Christianity. This only further incensed the emperor and he sentenced Catherine to death by spiked wheels (and artwork often depicts her with a wheel). Instead of tearing her apart, the wheels broke and injured onlookers. This was attributed to angels interceding but was only a temporary reprieve as she was ultimately beheaded.

"Patron Saint of Cooks and Comedians"

Saint Lawrence of Rome (225-258) was born in the northeast region of Spain (which was then part of a Roman province). As an archdeacon of Rome, he was charged with stewarding the Church's money and distributing alms among the poor.

St. Lawrence was doing this work during an exceptionally dark time in the Church's history. The Roman Emperor at the time, Valerian, was "kindly disposed towards the Christians" but as a ruler, he was "weak and irresolute, his abilities were unequal to the difficulties of the times." Valerian was persuaded to implement a severe edict in August of 258 that all bishops, priests, and deacons were to be executed immediately. [Löffler, K. (1912). Valerian. In *The*

Catholic Encyclopedia. New York: Robert Appleton Company. Retrieved November 22, 2022 from New Advent: *http://www.newadvent.org/cathen/15256b.htm*.]

Pope St. Sixtus II (c. 215-258), whom Lawrence greatly admired, and six of his deacons were rounded up and beheaded. St. Lawrence was martyred three days later. *Foxe's Book of Martyrs* (see "Recommended Reading" list at end of this book) attributes this quote to St. Lawrence as he was stretched on a bed of fire: "This side is now roasted enough, turn me, O tyrant, Decide whether you think roasted or raw is the better meat." (p. 74)

"The lost art of playing the fool"
Considered the Patron Saint of Holy Fools, Puppeteers, and Ventriloquists, **Saint Simeon**, sometimes referred to as Saint Simeon Salsus, was born in Syria during the sixth century and grew up in a wealthy family, "accustomed to every comfort and delusion." So it's interesting that he ultimately pursued the path of becoming a holy fool who shook loose the comforts and delusions of others.

Before he blazed a trail of folly, he spent 29 years living a hermit lifestyle with his good friend Saint John of Edessa. According to Leontus, the Bishop of Neapolis in the seventh century, in his hagiography, *The Life and Conduct of Abba Symeon Called the Fool for the Sake of Christ*, it was when the two friends first travelled to Palestine to become monks at the monastery of Saint Gerasimus, Simeon worried that his friend might abandon the austere lifestyle and return to his wife, cautioning, "… lest your boiling for your newlywed wife drag you away from this good path." I modified and incorporated this quote within the poem.

It will ultimately be Simeon who abandons John around the year 551 to head to the city of Emesa to heed a holy call to play the fool. His foolish works apparently kept neighbors from fornicating and stealing each other's goats. You can read the translation of Leontus' hagiographic work thanks to Derek Krueger. (Krueger, Derek. *Symeon the Holy Fool: Leontius's Life and the Late Antique City.* Berkeley: University of California Press, c1996. *http://ark.cdlib.org/ark:/13030/ft6k4007sx*)

While a number of images of the saint show him with a dead dog tied around his waist, other images portray Simeon holding a puppet that he used to mock himself and point out the foolishness of others. He's like the Forrest Gump of the sixth century, a divine idiot who holds up a mirror to the world around him.

Playing the fool seems a strange vocation but foolishness seems to tinge many saints' lives. John Saward, in his book *Perfect Fools* (Oxford: Oxford University Press, 1980), proposes this general rule, that "all saints are fools for Christ's sake, but some are called to be more foolish than others." Simeon definitely falls into the latter camp and is considered one of the first Holy Fools. Saward points out (on page 95) that folly "affirms God works through weakness, failure, and suffering and that the way to true life and joy is the way of the cross."

In trying to make sense of this path, Saward writes, "Folly for Christ's sake is a kind of dispossession, the surrender of worldly wisdom for Christ's sake, and thus is intimately connected with poverty ... To a world that 'clings', such dispossession seems foolish; by the standards of worldly astutia, such recklessness is insanity. No matter, for the poor man has already turned his back on that world and its wisdom. The monk has let go of every security, even the security of being of one mind with the world. The Christian must be poor in spirit, simple-hearted, and divinely foolish." (pp. 68 and 70).

"Nessie" and "Nessie, part two"
Saint Columba (521-597) was born in Ireland (where he is known as Saint Colmcille) and spent his adult life in Scotland. Depending on what sources you read, he either was banished by the king or he

exiled himself over a fight he had with his former teacher and another future saint, **Finnian of Movilla** (c. 495-589).

Finnian, Columba's former teacher, had a copy of the Vulgate, a Bible that had been translated into Latin by **Saint Jerome**. (See poem and note for "The cardinal has flown away.") Columba had copied a portion of the text when Finnian caught wind of it and demanded it be turned over to him. Columba refused and Finnian took the matter to the court. The verdict of this possibly first ever copyright dispute? The King of Ireland declared, "To every cow belongs her calf, to every book its copy." But when Columba still refused to turn it over, things got so out of hand that it incited a rebellion (now referred to as The Battle of the Books) that resulted in over 3,000 people dying. Unlike the 3,000 souls that perished, the manuscript survived and today is housed at the National Museum of Ireland.

"The tendency of nature is for things to protrude, leave home, and wander"
Saint Drogo (1105-1186) is quite busy as he is tasked with being the patron saint of many things: hernias, orphans, expectant mothers, shepherds, those others find unattractive, and for some reason I can't figure out, coffee.

Drogo was born in northern France (then known as Flanders) and lived way before coffee was introduced to Europe. So how does this humble shepherd become associated with coffee? While some coffee blogs have brewed up far-fetched ideas (such as busy baristas wish they too had Drogo's reported gift of bilocation so they could serve two customers at once), a 2015 article in *Crisis Magazine* ("Rediscovering Saint Drogo of Sebourg" by Christian E. O'Connell) notes that in an 1860 Belgium almanac, coffeehouse-keepers in the city of Mons (which is part of Belgium's Hainaut region and is a stone's throw from Sebourg and where Drogo lived out his days) associate Drogo with coffee. Drogo's habit of drinking only warm water, the article posits, might have led to this patronage.

"Perhaps also," O'Connell writes, "the early coffeehouse-keepers of Hainaut marveled at how the properties of the coffee bean are transformed by fire without being destroyed by it, and were reminded of Drogo's miraculous survival of the destruction of the church at Sebourg."

"Monica, you were bone to me"

Thanks to **Saint Monica**'s (331-387) son, **Saint Augustine**, and the book he wrote, *Confessions* (that I'm guessing today would be classified as a spiritual memoir), we know much about this fourth-century woman, at least from her son's perspective. After praying 17 years for her wayward child, Monica must have rejoiced in witnessing her son's conversion shortly before her death. If she had lived long enough to read his memoir, she would have loved many parts of it, like when Augustine, reflecting on his conversion, writes this most beautiful prayer: "You have made us for yourself, O Lord, and our heart is restless until it rests in you." I'm pretty sure, though, that she wouldn't have been pleased to learn that he had spilled the beans about her drinking problem, how at a young age and living with her parents, she was "avidly quaffing near goblets full of wine."

Monica gave up drinking and eventually married Patricius, only to endure an unhappy marriage complete with a cantankerous mother-in-law. But just like with her son, she didn't give up on her husband or his cranky mother and they, too, eventually left their bad behavior and paganism behind and embraced Christianity.

In my eight years at Saint Monica Elementary School, I don't ever recall learning that Monica was from Northern Africa, born in Thagaste (present-day Algeria). In portraits, statues, and other artwork (at St. Monica's and elsewhere), she was portrayed as lily white, but she wasn't, nor was her son.

But I do remember this: I was in third grade, sitting in Sister Genevieve's homeroom, when Murray McLaughlin, seated in front of me, turned around and told me that all churches named for a saint got a piece of the saint's bone to place somewhere in the building. "We got the biggest piece of her," he said. That seemed only fair to me since both our school and the church attached to it were named after Saint Monica. I wanted to know what bone and where it was, but Murray wasn't sure, thought maybe it was a leg bone in a wall or in the altar. Since he was an altar boy, I figured he had the inside scoop.

I'm grateful to artist Maxine Grippo for creating this gorgeous illustration to accompany "Monica, you were bone to me." (See Maxine's other illustration within this book for "Anatomy of prayer.")

"Saint of the Broom, help us learn your sweeping ways"
When he was a young boy growing up in Lima, Peru, **St. Martin de Porres** (1579-1639) apprenticed with a barber-surgeon and learned to cut hair and tend to the sick. He carried these skills with him into his years of service as a Dominican lay brother.

More than 300 years after his death, on May 6, 1962, he became the first canonized Black saint of the Americas. This was on the cusp of Vatican II, in which an ecumenical council would usher in sweeping changes to renew the Church and bring in much freshly needed air. The timing of his canonization was quite deliberate. According to Philip Kosloski's article, "Why St. Martin de Porres was canonized shortly before Vatican II," published in 11/3/22 in *Aleteia*, **Saint Pope John Paul XIII** (1881-1963) wanted to lift up this kind and humble saint as someone who captured the true spirit of Vatican II and served as an "example of how to live a life of holiness in the modern world."

"Dear Ursula of Archers, the Hun's arrow never flew"
The legend of this beautiful princess had been told and re-told through the centuries. How she acquired eleven thousand virginal maidens is a story in itself. According to some theories, a medieval

monk messed up while translating the legend, writing eleven thousand instead of eleven. It has also been posited that **Ursula** had a maiden named Undecimilla and that the monk confused this name with undicimila, meaning 11,000.

In 1969, the Vatican did quite a bit of ecclesiastical housecleaning and swept out a number of iffy saints from The Catholic Church's liturgical calendar, Saint Ursula among them.

Carol Cusack, a religion scholar at The University of Sydney, attempts to unpack this highly popular legend in "Hagiography and History: the Legend of Saint Ursula." In the fifteenth century, there developed a cult (not in the bad sense of brainwashing but of religious devotion) around Ursula. These were strained times as women were pushing to be actively involved in church missions and reform. Holding up this adventurous female saint as a role model could empower women "to defy authority, paternal, husbandly and ecclesiastical, in realizing their spiritual ambitions." For others who were not necessarily seeking a role model, "messages were conveyed about the power of the martyrs to intercede on behalf of the sinner, and to work miracles in the name of Christ."

"Anatomy of prayer"
There are four Jameses mentioned in the New Testament. Not to be confused with James the Great, **James the Just** (died around 69), also known as Old Camel Knees, is believed to be the brother of Jesus. **Saint Paul the Apostle** (c. 5-c. 65), in a letter to the Galatians, wrote: … *I went up to Jerusalem to get acquainted with Cephas and stayed with him fifteen days. I saw none of the other apostles—only James, the Lord's brother.*

While some scholars argue that they were cousins, whatever the relationship, around the year 42, James became an early leader who nurtured the Christian community in Jerusalem. It's also believed he wrote the epistle of James. Here's a good journal article about James: Scarborough, William J. "James the Just." *Journal of Bible*

and   Religion   9,   no.   4   (1941):   234–38.
http://www.jstor.org/stable/1459105.

Adored by her friends and family, **Jill the Cousin** (1964 -   ), also known as Jill the Nurturer, excels in the sacred vocation of motherhood. Known for her modesty, after being praised for her parenting of three beautiful children, Jill texted: *The mom thing is really hit or miss. Some days, one hits it out of the park. Other days, you can't find your bat!*

Jill approaches life and the curve balls it sends with joy, curiosity, and humor. Her family has attempted to capture her spirit in poems and paintings, but Jill escapes them. One day, she will become the Patron Saint of Parents, Trees, and Knees.

"Saint of Noticing Small Things"
Andrew, born in Galilee, was a brother of Simon Peter and most scholars think it's likely he was the younger of the two. While all four Gospels include the story of the feeding of the 5,000, it is only the Gospel of John that mentions Andrew's involvement in this event.

I found *The Galilean Fishing Economy and the Jesus Tradition* by K. C. Hanson (published in *Biblical Theology Bulletin* 27, 1997, 99-111) most helpful in getting a better sense of what it would have been like to be an ancient fisherman in Andrew's time.

In 62 A.D., he was crucified on an x-shaped cross, often referred to as Andrew's Cross. As the Patron Saint of Fishermen and Singers, Andrew is also considered the patron saint of many places, including Ukraine, Russia, Scotland, and Romania.

"Saint of Beekeepers and Beggars"
A heavy hitter in the saint world, **Saint Ambrose** (340-397) was a looming theological figure and social justice warrior of the 4th

century. This saint is also one of the four original doctors of the Catholic Church. Born and raised in Trier (present-day Germany), he became, rather against his wishes, Bishop of Milan in 374. As then governor of Italy's northern provinces, Ambrose was asked to lead the dialogue at an election meeting in hopes his presence might keep a riot from breaking out between the two camps of Christians—the Nicene Christians and the Arians—who were selecting a bishop to replace the Arian bishop who had died. As the *Vatican News* put it, "Just when the governor thought he had accomplished his mission successfully, the unexpected happened: from the crowd a child's voice rose loudly and found an echo in that of the entire assembly: 'Ambrose for our bishop!'"

Even though he wasn't interested in the job and, at that point, hadn't even been baptized Catholic, he was basically drafted by the people. That moment, and throughout much of his life, he seemed to have the ability to reach across aisles and gain the respect of those with remarkably different views.

One of his most admirable traits, I think, is how he both lived and preached justice for the poor. He said, "It is not from your own possessions that you are bestowing alms on the poor, you are but restoring to them what is theirs by right. For what was given to everyone for the use of all, you have taken for your exclusive use. The earth belongs not to the rich, but to everyone. Thus, far from giving lavishly, you are but paying part of your debt."

The common adage, "When in Rome, do as the Romans do" comes from Ambrose and has been condensed from his sage advice on how to follow local liturgical customs. What he said was, "When I am at Rome, I fast on a Saturday; when I am at Milan, I do not. Follow the custom of the church where you are, "When you are in Rome, live in the Roman style; When you are elsewhere, live as they live elsewhere."

Saint Monica (331-387) thought highly of Ambrose and saw him as an angel of God who uprooted her son from his former ways and led him to Christ. (See poem and note, "Monica, you were bone to me.")

"A nod to St. Nicholas"
Saint Nicholas (c. 270-343), better known in America as Santa Claus, was a bishop of Myra (in modern-day Turkey) in the fourth century. Some scholars believe he was one of the over 300 bishops who in 325 attended the Council of Nicea where the Nicene Creed (a profession of Christian faith and belief in one God) was first adopted.

The St. Nicholas Center, a non-profit organization in Michigan, has pulled together information, images, and documentaries on this saint, including details of a forensic study of Saint Nicholas and his ethnicity. You can check it out online at *www.stnicholascenter.org*.

"Since life is more than this blue cup and saucer"
In *The Legend of Saint Clare*, (a hagiography written shortly after her death and one that most scholars seem to think was authored by Franciscan Friar Thomas Celano who also wrote two hagiographies of St. Francis of Assisi), Clare's mother is on the verge of giving birth to her first of three daughters and is praying when she hears a voice boom, ""Do not be afraid, woman, for you will give birth in safety to a light which will give light more clearly than light itself." And so she names her newborn Chiara (Clare in English) which means *light*.

Born into a wealthy and noble Italian family, **Saint Clare** (1194-1253) lived up to her name. In 1212, at the age of eighteen, she detached herself from worldly things and her family's expectations to become the first woman to follow **St. Francis of Assisi** (c. 1181-1226). Many women would follow in her light. Her younger sister Agnes literally followed in her footsteps several weeks later. Clare would go on to found the first female order of Franciscans. Her sister Agnes helped establish a number of these Poor Clare homes throughout Italy. According to the website of the Poor Clare Sisters (*poorclare.org*), these 20,000 contemplative nuns are now in over 70 countries and are "surrounding the world with prayer."

The Legend of Saint Clare describes the saint as possessing "splendid optimism," a trait that most likely benefitted her as she doggedly pursued carving out a way for women to live the Franciscan lifestyle, a life of prayer, contemplation, simplicity, and poverty. While many miracles are attributed to Clare, perhaps the most astonishing one is that this woman fought the patriarchy of her day to accomplish reform *within* the church, an almost impossible feat then as it is now.

It's interesting to note that after Clare's father died, her mother **Ortolana** (unknown-c. 1238), sometimes referred to as Hortulana, entered the order established by her eldest daughter. Clare's youngest sister Beatrice (c. 1200-1260) also joined.

Clare was canonized a saint just two years after her death. Her sister **Agnes** (1197/8-1253) had to wait about five hundred more years to achieve sainthood in 1753. Their mother is considered Blessed by the Catholic Church, one step shy of canonization.

"Saint of the Blackbird"
While many legends—often revolving around animals and nature—have cropped up around this Irish saint, this one of **Saint Kevin** (c. 498-618) and the blackbird is my favorite. The bird is said to have landed on Kevin's palm on the first day of Lent. Given that Lent is the season of waiting, this seems only fitting that Kevin remains still, waiting for the bird's hatchlings to fly away.

By the time Kevin was twelve, he was living with monks. He eventually became a priest and went on to create a monastic community in Glendalough. By all accounts, he was a charismatic teacher and people came far and wide to seek his help and learn from him. When he could, he lived as a hermit in a cave (that today is known as Kevin's Bed). As his monastic community and popularity grew, he must have struggled to balance a life of solitude and community.

"The unfinished dance of the unreliable legend, St. Vitus"
Most of what has been passed down about **Saint Vitus** (c. 290-303) is the stuff of legends. What is known about this ancient saint, who is sometimes called Saint Guy, is that he was born in Sicily and martyred during the Christian persecution. He would have been 12 or 13 when he was killed. He is also considered one of the "14 Holy Helpers" of the Church. Another Holy Helper in this book is **Saint Denis**. (See poem and note for "Saint Denis of Migraines, be with us as we lose our way.")

"The exclamation point not yet invented"
Saint Simeon, born in Syria around 390, scrambled up a pillar (with a platform of around six feet) in 423 and supposedly stayed there until his death in 459. Simeon is sometimes referred to as Saint Simeon the Stylite as the Greek word for pillar is "stylos," from which the word stylite comes. Eventually, pillar life became passé and hermits who stood on them died.

Over the centuries, Simeon's pillar wore down and unfortunately, in 2016, the remains of Simeon's pillar along with the ancient monastery and church that was built near the pillar after his death were seriously damaged by a Russian airstrike. Some of the best images of these ancient ruins before the strike can be found in "Church of Saint Simeon Stylites, Aleppo, Syria," a post published in *Blue Lapis Road*, a travel blog. Here's the link:
bluelapisroad.wordpress.com/2020/07/26/qalaat-samaan-near-aleppo-syria.

Also, a note about notes: After writing "The exclamation point not yet invented," I came across an article by Vasilije Vranic ("The Cultural Influences on Stylitism as an Ascetic Practice: The Case of St. Simeon the Stylite" published in *Saint Vladimir's Theological Quarterly*, 63:3 (2019) 243-259.) Within a number of Vranic's 52 footnotes, he cited various publications from the Cistercian Studies Series which is published in Kalamazoo, Michigan! Western Michigan University, which is just a few miles down the road from where I live, houses the Medieval Institute and its Center for Cistercian and Monastic Studies.

The article itself was quite enlightening and offered a possible explanation as to why Simeon chose to live on a pillar. The author theorizes that Simeon would have been influenced by the Zoroastrian funeral practices of excarnation. This ancient religion held that the body was not to be buried or cremated but placed on platforms (that were built in isolated areas) so that it could be exposed to the elements. Also known as sky-burial, this practice would fit the saint's "pattern of ascetic mortification." By transcending the human condition and comforts of this earthly life, "The stylite is dead to the world … the stylite represents the risen Christ, the victor over death *par excellence*. Thus, the stylite's true *imitatio Christi* is his victory over death, as effected on the pillar/platform."

"Ceaseless is the work of saint and scientists in Russia's Los Alamos"
I managed to get one of my favorite quotes by **Saint Seraphim** (1754-1833) into this poem: "Acquire a peaceful spirit and thousands around you will be saved."

This Henry David Thoreau of the saint world lived much of his contemplative life in a tiny cabin deep in the Russian forest. In 1903, the Russian Orthodox Church deemed him a saint. Another of my favorite quotes from him that didn't make it into the poem is "You can never be too gentle, too kind."

"The Seven Sleepers of Ephesus"

I find the story of the **Seven Sleepers of Ephesus** (now modern-day Turkey), also known as Companions of the Cave, so appealing. This story has circulated for centuries in many languages and throughout Jewish, Christian, and Muslim communities. In fact, the Holy Qur'an devotes a section to this very story.

While researching saints, I've found many who give up sleep or sleep very little to show their love for God. The Seven Sleepers is a refreshing twist on the tale. The opposite of saints who sacrifice sleep, these sleepers first fell asleep in God around 250, during the reign of Decius. (A huge fan of paganism, this Roman emperor led violent assaults on Christians for not following his edict which ordered them to offer sacrifices to the Roman gods in front of a Roman official who would then sign a certificate to that effect.) When the sleepers arise two centuries later, Emperor Theodosius the Younger is in charge and the Roman Empire has co-opted Christianity.

The website, *CatholicSaints.Info.: notes about your extended family in heaven*, states that the translation of the story has led to confusion as "went to sleep in the Lord" was a common phrase that meant someone has died as a result of following their Christian faith. It is more likely, the site says, that they were tortured like other Christians of their day and then buried in the cave. Regardless, these sleepers survived the ignorance and onslaught of their time, and then slept their way into poems, plays, and books. They Rip Van Winkled their way into the waking world and combined neatly into one saint.

In 1969, the Seven Sleepers were stripped of their feast day by the Roman Catholic Church (considering it "purely imaginative romance") but are still celebrated twice a year in the Greek Orthodox Church on August 4 (date of their first sleep) and October 22 (date of their final and lasting sleep). To unearth more of this story, dig into "The Historicity of the Seven Sleepers," a blog post written by John Sanidopoulos. He made a pilgrimage to the archeological site of Ephesus and includes some interesting photos of the tombs and Cave of the Seven Sleepers. Here's the link: *www.johnsanidopoulos.com/2009/10/historicity-of-seven-sleepers-of.html*.

"I tell my mother about the Companions of the Cave"
See poem and note for "The Seven Sleepers of Ephesus."

"St. Genevieve, Patron Saint of Disasters, Fever, and Paris (c. 422-512)"
Saint Genevieve was born in Nanterre, near Paris. When she was seven years old, she briefly crossed paths with another saint, **Saint Germanus of Auxerre** (c. 378-448). This lawyer turned bishop was passing through her village on his way to England and it is said that he predicted her future sanctity.

Genevieve was quite well known in her day and even **Saint Simeon** who was around 70 at the time and perched on top of his pillar (see poem and note for "The exclamation point not yet invented") knew of her and asked merchants that were from her area to, upon their return, ask Genevieve to pray for him.

In "Religion, Subsistence, and Social Control: The Uses of Saint Genevieve," (*Eighteenth-Century Studies*, Vol. 13, No. 2, The Johns Hopkins University Press, Winter, 1979-1980, pp. 142-168) author Steven L. Kaplan lays out a number of times that Parisian authorities turned to Genevieve to dig their way out of a particular disaster. The saint was "sometimes rudely put to the test," such as in 1694 when she was called upon "to end the misery of famine; to halt the depredations of war; to end the ravages of disease." These government appeals for saintly aid were ultimately more political than spiritual. They wanted to "calm the public: to channel already mobilized and volatile passions into an innocuous outlet, to convert the crowd into a congregation, and to transform terror into resignation or despair into hope."

"My mother mentions in passing that I was held by a saint"

Born in Midland, Pennsylvania in 1914, **Father John Hardon** made his way to Kalamazoo, Michigan, to serve as an associate professor of Religion at Western Michigan University from 1962-67. He and my father struck up a friendship and in 1965, the same year that Lyndon B. Johnson signed the Voting Rights Act into law, he visited our home and held me. While my mother recalled what she served that evening for dinner, she couldn't remember what they drank. "Back then we didn't drink wine," she said. He may have just had water as, in *Moral Theology*, he dedicated an entire chapter to "Drinking and Temperance."

He would go on to hob nob with a number of prominent Catholics and future saints like **Mother Teresa**, Cardinal Joseph Ratzinger (later Pope Benedict XVI), and **Pope St. John Paul II**. He championed Catholic doctrine and orthodoxy and wrote over forty books on religion and theology, including "The Modern Catholic Dictionary" which he packed with over 5,000 terms of Catholic faith, worship, morals, history, and spirituality.

Father Hardon died in 2000 of bone cancer. In 2005, his canonization process began. An official website has been established (*hardonsj.org*) for the purpose of praying for his sainthood. He is currently deemed "A Servant of God," step one in the four-step process as the Church investigates a potential saint. If Father Hardon reaches step two, he will be declared Venerable, beatification follows, and he will then be assigned Blessed. If he moves on from this, he will be canonized a Saint. A post written by Jim Graves and published on the blog of the National Catholic Register on January 27, 2017, goes into detail about Hardon's possible canonization. Here's that link: *www.ncregister.com/blog/fr-john-hardon-may-be-on-his-way-to-canonization.*

"Saint Denis of Migraines, be with us as we lose our way"

Not much is known about **Saint Denis of Paris** (unknown-c. 250) other than that he was the first bishop of Paris and was beheaded in an area of France now called Saint-Denis. After he was martyred, a number of accounts say that his body was thrown in the river, fished out later by his followers, and buried. Obviously, this conflicts with the legend that he carried his decapitated head for six miles before falling to the ground.

Saint Denis is one of 14 saints who makes up the "14 Holy Helpers." This sacred squad was often called upon for help as the Black Plague raged through Europe from 1346 to 1349. **Saint Vitus** is also included with these 14 Holy Helpers. (See poem, "The unfinished dance of the unreliable legend, St. Vitus.")

"An admirable virgin of advanced age"
As a deaconess in the third century, **Apollonia** (unknown-249) preached throughout Alexandria, Egypt. She converted many to Christianity before becoming a martyr for refusing to renounce her faith. She is considered the Patron Saint of Dentists as well as those suffering from toothaches and other dental problems. In artwork, such as the image that follows the poem, she is often portrayed with pincers.

"After shoveling not quite five minutes"
Saint Sebaldus, who was probably born in England and died around 770, was a much-loved missionary in the Reichswald area of Germany. Even after he retired, he continued to pray and preach.

Unlike Saint Sebaldus, my fourth great-grandmother, Freelove Potter, had no talent for turning icicles into firewood. In January of 1823, as she stumbled through Maine woods searching for her children, no cottage appeared, nor the family cow that had gone missing earlier that day. Only white pines kept her company. Shaggy with snow, they had not yet transformed into beams and boards and ships and sailed away. When her husband Stinson came home from logging that day and discovered the cabin empty, he headed back out in search of his family. He found the children and brought them home. Meanwhile, Freelove trudged into the deep night and walked along a frozen lake. Most likely confused from severe hypothermia, she kept walking when the ice cracked and sliced the skin on her feet and ankles. The next day, not far from the lake, in a forest of black spruce and Penobscot pine, Freelove's body was found.

"A soft, unmuscled God"

Around 1400, images of this fictitious folk hero—a Jesus figure with beard and sometimes breasts and flaming hips—started cropping up in churches in Germany, France, Spain, Italy, England, and elsewhere. Known as **Saint Wilgefortis** (from the Latin phrase *virgo fortis*, meaning "strong virgin"), the English referred to this Christ-like woman as Unncumber. She was particularly popular with unhappily married women, so much so that **Saint Thomas More** (1478-1535) wrote "they reckon that for a peck of oats she will not fail to uncumber them of their husbands."

Until I started digging into the lives of saints, I had been a bit judgy and assumed that those living during medieval times were, for the most part, backwards. However, if Saint Wilgefortis is any kind of enlightenment barometer, it seems that the medieval faithful embraced a more complex understanding of the Divine than I realized. People may have connected with this bearded saint and uncovered a way to pray to God precisely because of her gender-blending appearance. Seeing the Christ-like Wilgefortis as genderqueer, genderfluid—or whatever label we might slap on this saint these days—might have felt particularly freeing for women and the LGBTQ community (though they wouldn't have known or necessarily identified with that label then). Meditating on her story and the image of a Christ-like woman *trans*-cending her circumstances might have led them to a deeper understanding of God, one that transcends gender and the societal expectations that go with it. Though only a legend, my guess is that Saint Wilgefortis uncumbered people from more than just bad husbands.

If you are interested in delving more deeply into this bearded saint, I suggest reading Lewis Wallace's "Bearded Woman, Female Christ: Gendered Transformations in the Legends and Cult of Saint Wilgefortis." *Journal of Feminist Studies in Religion* 30, no. 1 (2014): 43–63. In this fascinating article, Wallace states early on (page 44) that he is focused on "what Saint Wilgefortis *does* as a symbol, rather than what she *is*." For example, he notes that "Virgin martyrs were petitioned frequently enough for assistance with marriages, but Uncumber's seems to be the only cult on record focused on losing, rather than gaining, a husband." (p. 57)

"Resurrection here, among the tombs"
Of the more than 40 catacombs that have been discovered, one of the most intriguing is the Catacomb of Priscilla, named after **Saint Priscilla** (birth and death dates unknown), sometimes referred to as Prisca. She and her husband **Saint Aquilla** (birth and death dates unknown) were Jewish tentmakers and were friends with **Saint Paul** (c. 5-c. 65) who also was a tentmaker. They had met Paul the Apostle in Corinth after Emperor Claudius had banned Jews from living in Rome. A number of scholars believe that it was in Corinth that Paul converted them to Christianity. When the saintly couple eventually returned to Rome, they also used their home as a church. In Romans 16, 3-4, Paul says, "Greet Prisca and Aquilla, my fellow workers in Christ Jesus, who risked their necks for my life, to whom not only I but also all the churches of the Gentiles give thanks; greet also the church in their house." Some versions of the Bible translate "fellow workers" as "helpers" or "co-workers." Regardless, it seems to me that Paul saw both Priscilla and her husband as equals.

It is in a room of the Catacomb of Priscilla, known as the "Cubiculum of the Veiled Woman," three scenes of a particular woman's life are depicted. The middle image is largest and she is veiled and wearing what looks to be a priestly stole, her arms lifted as if she is preaching.

In another area, "The Greek Chapel," a fresco depicts what looks to be seven women celebrating the Eucharistic with one of the figures breaking the bread. In "The Secrets of the Santa Priscilla Catacombs" (an article by Amanda Ruggeri that was published in *BBC.com* on February, 24, 2015), upon the fresco's discovery, the assumption was that "if that figure is breaking bread, then he has to be male, because women wouldn't break bread and be leading the Eucharist," says Nicola Denzey Lewis, professor of religious studies at Brown University and the author of *The Bone Gatherers: The Lost Worlds of Early Christian Women*. Perhaps to aid that interpretation, in the 19th Century, she says, someone rubbed off some of the face's pigment, making it look shadowed, as if it has a beard. Yet thanks to the figures' dress (one figure in the middle even wears a veil, as a Roman woman would) and their delicate features, few academics today, or even visitors, think the figures are male."

Groups such as the Association of Roman Catholic Woman Priests say that these ancient scenes are evidence of females serving as priests in the early Church. The Vatican discounts these interpretations as "fairy tales." Whatever the case, women most definitely played a "large and in charge" role during the early beginnings of Christianity.

Thanks to Google Maps, you can take a virtual tour of some of Priscilla's underground labyrinth that meanders eight miles beneath Rome. Also, the International Catacomb Society maintains a website (*www.catacombsociety.org*) with loads of information, including links to Christian and Jewish catacombs.

"Patron Saint of Difficult Marriages"
St. Hedwig of Silesia (1174-1243) birthed seven (some sources say only six) children and outlived all but her daughter Gertrude. Hedwig was responsible for bringing the Cistercian Order to Silesia. She had a monastery and several churches built in the region. After the death of her husband in 1238, Hedwig went to live out the rest of her life in the Cistercian convent in Silesia, Poland, that she and

her husband had founded in 1203 and where their daughter Gertrude served as the abbess. Today, this monastery is known as Trzebnica Abbey as well as the Sanctuary of St. Jadwiga. **St. Jadwiga** (1373-1399) is also known as Hedwig, but it is not the Hedwig which this poem is based upon. (I probably should have also written a poem about St. Jadwiga as she was the first woman to be crowned as monarch of the Kingdom of Poland, reigning from 1384 until her death in 1399.)

Hedwig and her husband are both buried in one of the churches connected to this monastery. According to a 2019 article in the *Catholic News Agency* ("This princess saint was not Harry Potter's owl: St. Hedwig of Silesia" written by Hannah Brockhaus), the monastery is still active and considered to be Central Europe's largest existing 13th-century building.

St. Hedwig is also the aunt of **Saint Cunigunda**. (See poem and note for "Cunigunda, the Slapping Saint.")

"Daily mortification, prescription for the soul"
As of this writing, **Matt Talbot** (1856-1925), beatified in 1975, is halfway to official sainthood. He is considered the Patron of Struggling and Recovering Addicts and Alcoholics.

To learn more about Matt Talbot, check out this resource site which contains a variety of information, including a 1963 documentary of interviews with people who knew him: *http://venerablematttalbotresourcecenter.blogspot.com.*

"Saint Gemma Galgani, Daughter of Passion (1876-1903)"
Artist Michael Dunn, after producing a series of graphite drawings, asked me and some other poets to write poems in response to his work. (The poems were then displayed alongside Michael's work at the Kalamazoo Book Arts Center during the month of November 2017.)

In looking over Dunn's series, "Accidental Markings, No. 153" immediately grabbed me. I couldn't help but see **Saint Gemma** in the upside-down figure.

Only weeks before, I had been reading about Saint Gemma, one of eight children born into an Italian family. She recounts in her diary one of her earliest memories. She is not quite seven when her mother dies of tuberculosis, the very disease that will end Gemma's own life when she is 28. She couldn't seem to catch a break. When she was a teen, her father, a pharmacist, died, and she did her best to raise her siblings. She had desired to be a nun but due to poor health (she contracted meningitis at one point), was not accepted. Gemma recounts in her diary that it was June 8, 1935 that she first experienced the marks of the stigmata. "At that moment Jesus appeared with all his wounds open. But blood no longer came out of those wounds. Rather, flames as of fire issued forth from them and in a moment those flames came to touch my hands, feet and heart. I felt as if I would die."

Saint Gemma's diary, her biography and other writings, along with a number of pictures can be found at *StGemmagalgani.com*. And for a $20 donation, you can receive a relic locket that is said to contain a fragment of wood from St. Gemma's coffin. Here's a photograph of Saint Gemma:

Jules Ernest Livernois (Canadian, 1851-1933)

The first saint known to have stigmatas (the five wounds of Christ that appear on the body and bleed at times) was **Saint Francis of Assisi** (c. 1181-1226). A group of cultural historians (Tine Van Osselaer, Andrea Graus, and Leonardo Rossi) who research stigmatas like the kind Saint Gemma displayed, don't concern themselves with proving or disproving the veracity of these claims. Instead, they focus their research on what the stigmatas meant to people at that time. In one of their projects, *The Devotion and Promotion of Stigmatics in Europe, c. 1800–1950: Between Saints and Celebrities,* this team says that it's not until the 19th century that stigmatics—overwhelmingly young women from poor rural Catholic areas—become an actual thing. "The stigmatic type was aligned with contemporary popular ideas of what sanctity was – although these were not the ideas of the Church – with a focus on the miraculous body as proof of the divine. They were the religious celebrities of their time. Their fame was marketable and knowledge about them spread through the modern media." (p. 3)

My father once recounted a story to me how in 1952 he visited the village of Konnersreuth in Bavaria, Germany to see **Theresa Neumann** (1898-1962), a German mystic and stigmatic. Like Saint Gemma, she was poor, lived in a rural Catholic area, and became a stigmatic at a young age. If my memory is accurate, my father, accompanied by one of his army buddies, said that this saintly celebrity of her time was in bed in the home she had grown up in and her hands were bandaged so he couldn't see the wounds. He was one of many who travelled from all over to see her, and those who managed to visit on Good Friday could witness her wounds weeping. He was told by someone there (a French nun?) that she hadn't had anything to eat, other than Holy Communion, for something like 40 years. My father left the village that day not entirely sure what to think—was this for real or was it a hoax?—, but he did buy a book about her.

In 2005, the formal process of beatification for Neumann was initiated and currently considered Venerable, she is inching closer to sainthood.

"Underwater Jesus"
In 1956, on his fifteenth birthday, Gerald Schipinski drove a tractor out onto the field on his family's farm located near Bad Axe, Michigan. His father had asked him to shoot some crows so he took along his birthday present, a new shotgun. Later, his father noticed that the tractor was not moving and soon discovered that the gun had accidently slipped and killed Gerald. In Gerald's memory, his parents commissioned a crucifix for their son's grave. When the 11-foot crucifix finally arrived from Italy, it was broken. They refused to pay for the damaged God.

The crucifix was put up for auction and the marble Jesus went to the highest bidder: the Wyandotte Superior Marine Diving Club. They coughed up fifty dollars and after sinking more money into repairs, submerged it in 1962 in Little Traverse Bay which is off of Lake Michigan in the northern area of Michigan's Lower Peninsula. Years later, another Michigan diving club removed it from the water to make further repairs and in 1986 re-sunk it in a shallower spot, where it currently resides about 800 feet from the shore of Little Traverse Bay in Petoskey, Michigan. Today it serves as a memorial for divers who have lost their lives in the Great Lakes.

If the weather cooperates and the ice is thick enough (usually end of February or early March), people can view the crucifix. More information about this can be found on the *Petoskeyarea.com* website. You can also watch this two-minute clip created by Alex Childress to view this underwater Jesus for yourself: *www.facebook.com/AlexChildressPhoto/videos/215896700774822 2.*

"Back when I was a seven-year-old saint"

The two italicized phrases in this poem are attributed to the five-foot powerhouse of a saint, **Saint Teresa of Calcutta** (1910-1997). Also known as Mother Teresa, she founded the Missionaries of Charity, a group of women dedicated to serving the poor.

During her canonization mass on September 4, 2016, Pope Francis said, "She bowed down before those who were spent, left to die on the side of the road, seeing in them their God-given dignity. She made her voice heard before the powers of this world, so that they might recognize their guilt for the crime of poverty they created."

"Unpacking the hazelnut"
When **Julian of Norwich** (1342/3-c. 1416) was just a child, the Black Death visited her English village of Norwich. It's estimated that the population of Norwich—which had been around 25,000—was 5,000 by 1348. By 1351, the Black Death had wiped out as much as an estimated 60 percent of the European population. In 1373, Julian became extremely ill and was on the verge of death. During this time, she had 16 visions and when she recovered, she wrote about them in what is now known as the "Short Text." A decade or so later, she wrote about the experience in greater depth. This "Long Text," known as *Revelations of Divine Love,* is the first book known to have been written in English by a woman.

This poem was inspired by one of Julian's sixteen visions. In *Revelations of Divine Love,* she writes: "He shewed me a little thing the quantity of a hazel-nut, in the palm of my hand; and it was as round as a ball. I looked thereupon with eye of my understanding, and thought, What may this be? And it was answered generally thus: It is all that is made. I marvelled how it might last, for me thought it might suddenly have fallen to naught for littleness. And I was answered in my understanding: It lasteth, and ever shall, for that God loveth." (p. 10)

Around 1390 or thereabouts, Julian became an anchoress. Prior to being enclosed in a small room or cell attached to the outside of the church, a funeral-type service was probably held, as was custom for those anchoresses (women) or anchorites (men) choosing to be dead to the world and spend the rest of their life in prayer and contemplation. The service would have been incorporated into a celebration of mass. If you want to know what a service for enclosing these holy persons involved, I'd suggest reading this 2019 article by Luke Ayers and Victoria Bahr of Trinity University: "A twelfth-century service for enclosing an anchorite or anchoress: Introduction, Latin text, and translation." *The Expositor: A Journal of Undergraduate Research in the myHumanities*, 14, 1-12.

St. Drogo, another saint in this book, was also an anchorite. See poem and note for "The tendency of nature is for things to protrude, leave home, and wander."

If you are interested in learning more about anchoresses and anchorites as well as exploring Julian of Norwich's work, check out *Discovering Literature: Medieval* that is available online thanks to The British Library. The website is: *https://www.bl.uk/medieval-literature.*

As of this writing, Julian of Norwich is not officially considered a saint in the Catholic Church but she does have a May 13th feast day. And Julian's Feast Day is celebrated on May 8th by Anglican and Lutheran churches.

"Patron Saint of the Selfish, who once wore the most exquisite clothes"
By the time of her death, **Saint Jeanne Delanoue** (1666-1736), also known as Saint Joan of the Cross, had established a dozen communities of her Sisters throughout France who dedicated themselves to serving the poor and needy. The order she founded was later renamed Congregation of St. Anne of Providence.

It was not until 1982 that Saint Jeanne was canonized a saint by **Pope Saint John Paul II** (1920-2005). As pope, he was quite rambunctious in canonizing saints, 482 in total during his reign (1979-2005). Two other saints he canonized can be found in this book, **Saint Maximilian Kolbe** (see poem and note for "Numbered Our Days: Maximilian Kolbe") and **Jadwiga of Poland** (see note for "Patron Saint of Difficult Marriages").

"Take up thy snowball"
Born in 1380 in Schiedam, Holland, **Lidwina**, also referred to as **Saint Lydwine**, is considered the Patron Saint of the Chronically Ill and Ice Skaters. As a young girl, she fell on the ice while skating and broke a rib. Thereafter, her health declined. Throughout her life, this Dutch mystic suffered many ailments, including movement, balance, and vision problems, while also experiencing brief periods of remission, leading some scholars to believe she suffered from multiple sclerosis. She died in 1433 at the age of 53.

One hagiography that I found most helpful while working on this poem was *St. Lydwine of Schiedam, Virgin* by Thomas à Kempis (Burns & Oates, London, 1912). I especially enjoyed the titles that Kempis gave each chapter, like "Of the hardness of her bed, and the cold she suffered in winter" and "Of the opinion of a certain doctor, and the miracle that befell her."

Kempis' account is basically an edited and translated version of an earlier hagiography written by Friar John Brugman. Brugman wrote two lives of St. Lidwina. The first was published in 1433 and the second came out twenty-five years after his death, in 1498. The wood drawing image that accompanies this poem is from the latter edition.

See also, poem and note for "The ineffable sweetness of her milky glory."

"The ineffable sweetness of her milky glory"
Meander long enough through the life of saints, and you'll discover plenty of lactation stories involving Mother Mary's milk. Why this fascination with milk and breasts, I wondered? And then I stumbled upon **Lidwina**'s story, in which the saint, as relayed in the poem, basically nurses the widow Catherine. I initially found it hard to suspend my 21st century perspective: Lidwina, physically dependent upon Catherine, her caretaker, is in an abusive situation. However, I came across a scholarly piece ("Embodying the Saint: Mystical Visions, Maria Lactans and the Miracle of Mary's Milk," in *Matter of Faith: An Interdisciplinary Study of Relics and Relic Veneration in the Medieval Period*, J. Robinson, L. deBeer and A. Harndon, eds. [British Museum Research Publication 195, 2014]: 151-158) that helped me break through my modern perspective to grasp, however faintly, the medieval mindset for understanding these suckling saints.

The author, Dr. Vibeke Olson, an associate professor at University of North Carolina Wilmington, writes that the Middle Ages were rampant with milk relics, with some churches in Rome even claiming to have acquired drops of Mary's milk! From this time that is drenched in images of "Mary suckling the infant Christ, mystical visions of nursing or being nursed, accounts of miracles attributed to her milk, miracles as a form of imitation, prayers and poems celebrating Mary's breasts and milk to reliquaries containing the precious substance, one could say the period was quite literally awash in Marian milk."

Lidwina, born in 1380, was living during these abundantly milky times, so it shouldn't be surprising that visions of Mary, lactating virgins, and Lidwina's own lactating breasts are bound up in her story. But how would the medieval mind make sense of this? What would it mean?
Olson asserts that "Mary's milk, like Christ's sacrificial blood, was something that could be partaken of, or even in some cases miraculously produced, even if only in an imagined or visionary

experience. For that reason, it was not only a powerful devotional object that could be seen and touched, but also and perhaps more importantly it was a concrete manifestation of her physical being by means of its ingestibility and miraculous appearances, and the idea that devotees could quite literally embody the saint within themselves."

Also, refer to poem and note about St. Lidwina for "Take up thy snowball."

"Cunigunda, the Slapping Saint"
When this saint who goes by numerous names and spellings (such as Cunigunda of Luxembourg, Kunigunde, and Kinga) got married, her husband, then the Duke of Bavaria, gifted her with a castle in Bamberg. (When I got married, my husband gave me a t-shirt. I'm not complaining. It's my favorite gardening shirt and I've worn it for almost 20 years.)

Cunigunda (c. 975-1039) and **Henry II** (c. 973-1024), who eventually became King of Germany (in 1002) and King of Italy (in 1004), gave away much of their wealth. Over the course of their marriage, they used their resources and positions of power to build a more peaceful and just world. When Henry II died, Cunigunda became a Benedictine nun, entering the very convent the couple had helped to build. Eventually, she moved into the role of Abbess.

Henry II was canonized a saint around 1146, and Cunigunda was canonized not long after, in 1200. During her canonization process it was reported that she performed nineteen miracles, many of them related to helping children. Cunigunda, who also happens to be a descendant of Charlemagne, is considered the patron saint of a number of places, including Lithuania, Luxembourg, Poland, and the Diocese of Bamberg (in Germany). Cunigunda's aunt, **St. Hedwig**, is also featured in this book. (See poem and note for "Patron Saint of Difficult Marriages.")

"The sad and disturbing story of eleven-year-old Maria Goretti (1890-1902)"

Saint Maria is one in a long line of females on the verge of being raped and hailed as heroes for thwarting their attackers, the sainting solidifying the myth that "defiled," a woman is useless; deflowered, she could never bloom.

When Maria became the youngest person canonized a saint on June 24, 1950, her mother was in attendance. While widely circulated that Maria's murderer also attended, I don't believe that to be the case, as the associated press, which covered the event, specifically noted that Alessandro was not present.

"Saint Thecla and the monk seals"

Born into a prominent family in Iconium (now Konya, Turkey), **Saint Thecla** (c. 30-first century) (sometimes spelled Thekla) had a huge following of women throughout Asia Minor and Egypt. Thecla was one of a number of female leaders conspicuously present and growing the Jesus movement in the early church by preaching, baptizing, and carrying out liturgical ceremonies.

Sometime after Thecla's death, written narratives known as *The Life of Thecla* and *Acts of Thecla* (the later text morphing into *Acts of Paul and Thecla*) began circulating about her preaching, converting, and healing works. Written in Greek, an English translation of *Acts of Paul and Thecla* is available online in the Ante-Nicene Christian Library.

One ancient woman, Ergeria, who visited one of Thecla's shrines in 384 wrote about her experience in her journal. "In God's name I arrived at the martyrium, and we had a prayer there, and read the whole Acts of holy Thekla." Some, though, weren't as enthused with Thecla and her acts. As. Dr. Ally Kateusz points out in her enlightening book, *Mary and Early Christian Women: Hidden Leadership* (London: Palgrave Macmillian, 2019), the early Christian writer Tertullian (c.155-c. 220) complained about Thecla and how her example was giving other women license to preach and baptize. A little over 200 years later, **Pope Saint Gelasius** would come along and condemn the *Acts of Paul and Thecla* as apocryphal. (See note for "Three Black Popes.") Saint Thecla is just one example Dr. Kateusz provides of how women who were leaders within the early church were redacted and sometimes even erased in later texts.

In addition to the text, several images of Thecla exist to this day. In 1906, two sixth century images of Thecla and Paul were uncovered in a cave off the coast of Turkey. And while the Catholic Church may have tossed Thecla aside, the Greek Church still considers her a "protomartyr among women and equal to the Apostles" and celebrates her feast day on September 24.

To learn more about Thecla, I recommend Susan E. Hylen's *A Modest Apostle: Thecla and the History of Women in the Early Church* (Oxford University Press, 2015).

"Relics of the flesh"
Because of her dynamic leadership and profound theological writings, not to mention the work she put into founding and reforming convents throughout Spain, **Saint Teresa of Avila** (1515-1582), along with **Saint Catherine of Siena** (1347-1380), was declared a Doctor of the Catholic Church in 1970. They are, as of this writing, the first and only two women to hold this title.

One of Saint Teresa's traits I most admire: her sense of humor and ability to not always take herself seriously, something that seems to be a chronic hazard in the saint occupation. My favorite story that illustrates this is when one of the younger nuns who lived in her convent finds Teresa in the kitchen chowing down on some tasty partridge. The nun is horrified and wonders aloud what people might think given it was during a time of fasting and abstinence from meat. "Let them think whatever they want," said Teresa. "There's a time for penance, and a time for partridge."

Within her writings about prayer and her understanding of the Divine, she also included her thoughts, feelings, and described her bodily experiences, including visions, loss of consciousness, and chronic headaches. While she has been labeled a 'patroness of hysterics' by some, recent scholarly work suggests that she may have suffered from ecstatic epileptic seizures, a rare form of epilepsy. (During these episodes, which are often imperceptible to others, the person may feel a sense of bliss, enhanced physical well-being, and heightened awareness of self or the external world.)

One of the more interesting articles I've come across approaches Teresa's life and writings from the perspective of feminist disability theories. Written by Professor Juárez-Almendros, faculty member of the Disability Studies Forum at the University of Notre Dame, she points out that if we approach Teresa from a purely scientific or faith-filled position, we limit ourselves on coming to a deeper understanding of this most extraordinary woman. ("Hallucinations, Persecutions and Self-Defense: The Autobiography of Teresa of Ávila" by Encarnación Juárez-Almendros *Arizona Journal of Hispanic Cultural Studies, Volume 17*, 2013, pp. 177-192.)

"Three Black Popes"
Pope Saint Victor (c. 155-199) was the first person from the African continent to serve as pope. As the 14th pope, he reigned from 189 to 198, when he was most likely martyred for his faith. He's also the first pope who started writing church documents and celebrating mass in Latin, rather than Greek.

Pope Saint Miltiades (unknown-314), also known as Melchiades the African, was the 32nd pope and reigned from 311 to 314. He signed Emperor Constantine's laws that ended persecutions and established Christianity as the religion of the Roman Empire. It was **Saint Augustine** who referred to Miltiades as "a true son of peace" and I slightly modified this description to include within the poem.

Hundreds of **Pope Saint Gelasius's** (410-496) writings survive. As 49th pope, he greatly influenced the view of the papacy's supreme authority for centuries to come. "There are," he wrote, "two powers by which this world is chiefly ruled: the sacred authority of the priesthood and the authority of kings."

He is credited with saving Rome from famine, offering up both his and the Church's resources to help those in need. We (and Hallmark) can also thank Pope Gelasius for establishing the Feast Day of February 14th for the much-celebrated saint and martyred bishop, **Valentine** (c. 226-c. 269). However, he apparently wasn't a fan of **Saint Thecla** (c. 30-first century) as he condemned the *Acts of Paul and Thecla* as apocryphal. (See poem and note for "Saint Thecla and the monk seals.")

"Numbered our days: Maximilian Kolbe"
When my mother told me that **Maximilian Kolbe** (1894-1941) was one of her favorite saints, I had to look into his story and write a poem about this Franciscan friar who volunteered to die in place of a stranger. As Patron Saint of our Difficult Century, he is probably very busy.

"The cardinal has flown away"
While **Saint Jerome**'s (c. 347-419) scholarly and aesthetic life has been portrayed throughout the centuries by numerous artists, this poem was inspired by Joos Van Cleve's "St. Jerome in Penitence," painted around 1516 and housed at the Muskegon Museum of Art.

A prolific writer, Jerome may be best known for translating the Hebrew Bible into Latin. Born in Crotia (a Roman province that is seated in today's Bosnia) and educated in Rome, Jerome is the Patron Saint of Librarians, Translators, and Encyclopedists. For a time, he served as librarian and secretary to Pope Damasus. He might have been pope himself, if not for his sarcastic humor and temper, often aimed at Roman clergy. Not surprisingly, when Pope Damasus died, Jerome was kicked out of Rome. He ended up in

Bethlehem and continued writing and translating the Bible. Known as the Vulgate, this translation into the "vulgar" or everyday Latin made the Bible accessible to the common people. Still used by the Catholic Church today, his translation set the standard for the King James version.

This huge undertaking would not have been possible without the help of two women, **Saint Paula** (347-404), a wealthy widow, and her daughter **Saint Eustochium** (c. 368-c. 420). While Paula helped out his endeavors financially, both women collaborated with him on his scriptural translations and commentaries. He held them in high esteem and their support meant everything to Jerome, as evidenced by one of many letters he wrote them. In one letter from 390, he wrote, "Therefore, I beseech you, Paula and Eustochium, to pour out your supplications for me to the Lord, that so long as I am in this poor body, I may write something pleasing to you, useful to the Church, worthy of posterity. As for my contemporaries, I am indifferent to their opinions, for they pass from side to side as they are moved by love or hatred."

The 17th Century Spanish painter Francisco de Zurbarán created an oil on cloth image of these three saints:

Francisco de Zurbarán (Spanish, 1598-1664)
"Saint Jerome with Saint Paula and Saint Eustochium, c.
1640/1650"
Samuel H. Kress Collection, Courtesy of the National Gallery of
Art, Washington

Together, they also raised a convent (which Paula oversaw, and when she died, her daughter took over), a monastery (that Jerome oversaw), a church, and a hospice/hotel for those who came from all over the world to make pilgrimages to holy places. "In our monastery," wrote Jerome, "hospitality is our priority, and we welcome with the cheerful face of kindness all who come. For we want to make sure that Mary and Joseph find shelter in the inn and that Jesus not be shut out and say to us: 'I was a stranger and you did not welcome me.'"

When Rome fell in 410 and refugees were fleeing, he wrote, "I have put aside all my study to help them. Now we must translate the words of the Scriptures into deeds, and instead of speaking holy words, we must do them."

Three sources that were instrumental in helping me think about Jerome:

"The Principal Works of Jerome," compiled and accessible online here: *http://www.documentacatholicaomnia.eu/03d/1819-1893,_Schaff._Philip,_3_Vol_06_Jerome,_EN.pdf.*

"Jerome's Epitaphium Paulae: Hagiography, Pilgrimage, and the Cult of Saint Paula," Andrew Cain, *Journal of Early Christian Studies*, Johns Hopkins University Press, Volume 18, Number 1, Spring 2010, pp. 105-139.

"Rembrandt's Tree Stump: An Iconographic Attribute of St. Jerome," Susan Donahue Kuretsky, *The Art Bulletin*, Dec., 1974, Vol. 56, No. 4 (Dec., 1974), pp. 571-580.

A listing of the saints included within the poems and/or notes in this book, in order of their feast days:

January 2
Saint Seraphim (1754-1833)
Patron Saint of Nuclear Weapons

January 2
Blessed Ortolana of Assisi (unknown-c. 1238)

January 3
Saint Genevieve (c. 422-512)
Patron Saint of Disasters, Fever, and Paris

January 10
Saint Pope Miltiadis (unknown-314)
Patronage unknown

January 15
Paul the Hermit (c. 230-341)
Patron Saint of Children, San Pablo City, the Philippines, and the Order of Saint Paul the First Hermit

January 18
Saint Priscilla (unknown-first century)
Patron Saint of Strong Marriages and Love

January 18
Saint Aquilla, husband of Saint Priscilla (unknown-first century)
Patron Saint of Strong Marriages and Love

January 26
Saint Paula (347-404)

Patron Saint of Widows

February 9
Saint Apollonia (unknown-249)
Patron Saint of Dentists and Those Dealing with Dental Problems

February 14
Saint Valentine (unknown-c. 1226)
Patron Saint of Love, Lovers, Engaged Couples, Happy Marriages, and the Mentally Ill

March 17
Saint Gertrude of Nivelles (626-659)
Patron Saint of Cats and Gardeners

March 19
Saint Joseph, Husband of Mary (unknown-c. 18)
Patron Saint of Fathers, Immigrants, Working People, and House Sellers

April 11
Saint Gemma of Galgani (1878-1903)
Patron Saint of Pharmacists and Tuberculosis Patients

April 14
Saint Lidwina (1380-1433)
Patron Saint of Ice Skaters and the Chronically Ill

April 16
Saint Drogo (1105-1186)
Patron Saint of Hernias, Orphans, Expectant Mothers, Shepherds, Unattractive People, and Coffee.

April 29
Saint Catherine of Siena (1347-1380)
Patron Saint of Fire Prevention and Nurses

May 3
Saint James the Just (unknown-62)
Patronage unknown

May 13
Julian of Norwich (1342/3-c. 1416)
Note: Though not recognized as a saint in Catholic Church, she does have a feast day. And both the Anglican and Lutheran churches celebrate Julian's Feast Day on May 8. Some consider her the Patron of Cats.

June 3
Saint Kevin (c. 498-618)
Patron Saint of Blackbirds

June 7
Venerable Matt Talbot (1856-1925)
Patron of Struggling and Recovering Addicts and Alcoholics
Note: As not yet canonized, feast day not established, so noting June 7, his death date.

June 9
Saint Columba (c. 521-597)
Patron Saint of Poets, Floods, and Bookbinders

June 15
Saint Vitus (c. 290-303)
Patron Saint of Dancers, Actors, Epileptics, and Storms

June 22
Saint Thomas More (1478-1535)
Patron Saint of Adopted Children, Lawyers, Civil Servants, and Politicians

June 27
Seven Sleepers of Ephesus (considered a legend, first died in c. 250)
Note: This feast day is no longer celebrated by the Catholic Church. But "Seven Sleepers Day" is celebrated each year in Germany on June 27.

June 29
Saint Paul (c. 5-c. 65)
Patron Saint of Missionaries, Evangelists, Theologians, and Journalists

July 1
Saint Simeon Salsus (c. 522-unknown)
Patron Saint of Holy Fools, Puppeteers, and Ventriloquists

July 6
Saint Maria Goretti (1890-1902)
Patron Saint of Sexually Abused, Assault/Rape Victims

July 13
Saint Henry the Exuberant (c. 972-1024)
Patron Saint of the Benedictine Oblates

July 13
Saint Cunigunda (c. 975-1040)
Patron Saint of Lithuania, Pregnant Women, and Sick Children

Note: Feast day originally celebrated on March 3 but it was changed to coincide with her husband's (Saint Henry the Exuberant) feast day.

July 17
Saint Jadwiga (1373-1399)
Patron Saint of Queens and Poland

July 20
Saint Wilgefortis (legend, started around 1350)
Patron Saint of Trans People, the Unhappily Married, Abused Women, and Musicians

July 21
St. John of Edessa (6th century)
Patronage unknown

July 28
Saint Pope Victor I (c.155-199)
Patronage unknown

August 7
Pope Saint Sixtus II (c. 215-258)
Patron Saint for the Prosperity of Grapes

August 10
Saint Lawrence of Rome (c. 225-258)
Patron Saint of Cooks and Comedians

August 11
Saint Clare of Assisi (1194-1253)
Patron Saint of Television, Laundry, Eye Disease, and Goldsmiths

August 14
Saint Maximilian Kolbe (1894-1941)
Patron Saint of Drug Addicts, Political Prisoners, Journalists, and Our Difficult Century

August 17
Saint Jeanne Delanoue (1666-1736)
Patron Saint of the Poor and Orphaned

August 17
Saint Hyacinth (c. 1185-1257)
Patron Saint of Weightlifters, Pierogi, and Those in Danger of Drowning

August 27
Saint Monica (c. 331-387)
Patron Saint of Mothers, Difficult Marriages, Alcoholics, and Abuse Victims

August 28
Saint Augustine (c. 354-430)
Patron Saint of Printers, Brewers, and Theologians

September 10
Saint Finnian of Movilla (c. 495-589)
Patron Saint of Ulster (an Irish province)

September 12
Saint Mary, Mother of Jesus (bce. 18-c. 48)
Patron Saint of Mothers, Children, and Humanity
Note: This feast day focuses on Mary as a person and she has, at least by my count, an additional 17 more feast days.

September 18
Venerable Theresa Neumann (1898-1962)
Note: As not canonized, feast day not established, so noting her death date.

September 23
Saint Thecla (c. 30-first century)
Patron Saint of Tarragona in Catalonia (Spain)
Note: Her feast day is no longer celebrated by the Catholic Church.

September 28
Saint Eustochium (c. 368-c. 419)
Note: Patronage unknown, but I think she should be considered Patron Saint of Translators.

October 4
Saint Francis of Assisi (c. 1181-1226)
Patron Saint of Animals and Ecology

October 9
Saint Denis of Paris (unknown-c. 250)
Patron Saint of Migraines, Headaches, and Hydrophobia

October 11
Pope Saint John Paul XIII (1881-1963)
Patron Saint of Christian Unity and other Popes Named John

October 17
Saint Hedwig (1174-1243)
Patron Saint of Difficult Marriages

October 21

Ursula of Archers (legend)
Patron Saint of School Girls
Note: Her feast day is no longer celebrated by the Catholic
Church.

October 22
Pope Saint John Paul II (1920-2005)
Patron Saint of Poland, Families, and Sports

October 28
Saint Jude (first century-c. 65)
Patron Saint of Hopeless Cases

November 3
St. Martin de Porres (1579-1639)
Patron Saint of Social Justice, Racial Harmony, Public Schools,
and Barbers

November 16
Saint Agnes of Assisi (c. 1197-1253)
Patron Saint of Chastity

November 18
Saint Juthwara of Cornwall (sixth century)
Patron Saint of Cheese

November 21
Saint Pope Gelasius (410-496)
Patronage unknown

November 22
Saint Cecilia (c. 130-230)
Patron Saint of Musicians

November 25

Saint Catherine of Alexandria (c. 287-305)

Patron Saint of Seamstresses, Potters, Nurses, and Craftspeople Using Wheels

December 6

Saint Nicholas (c. 270-343)

Patron Saint of Children, Sailors, Pharmacists, and the Falsely Accused

December 7

Saint Ambrose (c. 340-397)

Patron Saint of Beekeepers and Beggars

December 13

Saint Lucy (c. 283-304)

Patron Saint of the Blind

December 30

Servant of God John Hardon (1914-2000)

Note: As not yet canonized, feast day not established, so noting his death date. And if left up to me, I would make him the Patron Saint of Professors.

RECOMMENDED READINGS

Craughwell, Thomas. *This Saint's For You!* Philadelphia, PA: Quirk Book, 2007.

Craughwell, Thomas. *Saints Behaving Badly*. New York: Image, 2006.

Foxe, John, Paul L. Maier, and R.C. Linnenkugel. *Foxe's Book of Martyrs*. Grand Rapids, MI: Kregel Publications, 2016.

Hylen, Susan E. *A Modest Apostle: Thecla and the History of Women in the Early Church*. New York, NY: Oxford University Press, 2015.

Kateusz, Ally. *Mary and Early Christian Women: Hidden Leadership*. London: Palgrave Macmillan, 2019.

Law, Sarah. (Ed.) *All Shall Be Well: Poems for Julian of Norwich*. Amethyst Press, 2023.

Martin, James SJ. *My Life with the Saints.* Chicago, Illinois: Loyola Press, 2006.

McGinley, Phyllis. *Saint Watching*. New York: Viking, 1969.

Saward, John. *Perfect Fools: Folly for Christ's Sake in Catholic and Orthodox Spirituality*. Oxford: Oxford University Press, 1980.

Williams, Jerome K. *Saints for Our Times*. Greenwood Village, CO: Augustine Institute, 2017.

ACKNOWLEDGEMENTS

Many thanks to the editors of the following publications in which these poems first appeared:

Gyroscope Review, "An admirable virgin of advanced age"

Columbia Journal, "The pope must canonize a Patron Saint of Rats right now"

The Windhover, "Having bought St. Joseph, I bury him" and "Saint of the Blackbird"

Nimrod, "Searching." "Searching" later anthologized in *Mother Mary Comes to Me* (Madville Publishing) that was named one of the 2022 Books All Georgians Should Read by Georgia Center for the Book.

Nuclear Impact: Broken Atoms in Our Hands (a Shabda Press anthology), "Ceaseless is the work of saint and scientists in Russia's Los Alamos"

Immigration & Justice For Our Neighbors (a Celery City Books anthology), "Saint Denis of Migraines, be with us as we lose our way"

Harmony, "The tendency of nature is for things to protrude, leave home, and wander"

Amsterdam Quarterly, "Saint of the Broom, help us learn your sweeping ways"

A Beginner's Guide to Heaven (Unsolicited Press), "To All the B Saints." "Searching" and "Having bought St. Joseph, I bury him" also appeared in this book.

Deep Overstock, "Saint of Beekeepers and Beggars"

Ten Poems of Kindness, Volume 2 (a Candlestick Press pamphlet) published an earlier version of the third stanza of "A Nod to St. Nicholas." *Encore Magazine* later published the entire poem in their December 2023 issue.

All Shall Be Well (an Amethyst Press anthology), "Unpacking the hazelnut"

Garfield Lake Review, "Still life of party with lesser saints, many who refused to marry or have sex with rich, pagan kings"

EcoTheo Review, "Addressing the flaxen spirit, not yet linen" and "Linen women, with a nod to St. Catherine of Alexandria, Patron Saint of Seamstresses"

Belletrist, "Monica, you were bone to me"

Encore Magazine, "St. Genevieve, Patron Saint of Disasters, Fever, and Paris (422-512)"

Snakeskin, #278, the Cryptozoology issue, "Nessie"

The Last Girl's Club, "St. Thecla and the monk seals"

Poetry Society of Michigan newsletter, "After shoveling not quite five minutes"

The Offbeat, "Job Posting"

Saint Ambrose once said, "No duty is more urgent than that of returning thanks." So it is with deep appreciation that I also thank the following individuals/groups for their own unique contributions which helped shape this book:

To the awesome team at Unsolicited Press who champions the works of the unsung and underrepresented, profuse thanks for believing in my writing and including this book in your 2025 lineup of "women only" authors.

Dawgs, so grateful for your insightful critiques and encouragement throughout this saint project.

Michigan artists Maxine Grippo, Michael Dunn, and Garrylee McCormick, many thanks for allowing your brilliance to be nestled within this book.

Donna Carroll, much appreciation for reading these poems and notes and offering many helpful suggestions.

And, as always, John and Tom, your love and support keep me going.

ABOUT THE AUTHOR

Jennifer Clark is the author of three previous poetry collections: *A Beginner's Guide to Heaven* (Unsolicited Press), *Necessary Clearings*, and *Johnny Appleseed: The Slice & Times of John Chapman* (both published by Shabda Press). She is also the author of the children's book *What Do You See In Room 21 C?* and the co-editor of the anthology, *Immigration & Justice For Our Neighbors* (both Celery City Books). Her most recent book, *Kissing the World Goodbye*, ventures into the world of memoir, braiding family tales with recipes. Published by Unsolicited Press, it made their list for "Top Selling Books of 2022."

Clark's poems, essays, and fiction have appeared in numerous literary journals, magazines, and anthologies. Her work has received seven Pushcart Prizes nominations (in poetry, fiction, and nonfiction) and has been nominated for "Best of the Net," "Best Microfiction," and a Rhysling Award. She lives in Kalamazoo, Michigan, with her husband John and son Tom. Her website is *jenniferclarkkzoo.com.*

ABOUT THE PRESS

Unsolicited Press is based out of Portland, Oregon and focuses on the works of the unsung and underrepresented. As a womxn-owned, all-volunteer small publisher that doesn't worry about profits as much as championing exceptional literature, we have the privilege of partnering with authors skirting the fringes of the lit world. We've worked with emerging and award-winning authors such as Amy Shimshon-Santo, Brook Bhagat, Elisa Carlsen, Tara Stillions Whitehead, and Anne Leigh Parrish.

Learn more at unsolicitedpress.com. Find us on Instagram, X, Facebook, Pinterest, Bsky, Threads, YouTube, and LinkedIn. Unsolicited Press also writes a snarky newsletter on Substack.

www.ingramcontent.com/pod-product-compliance
Lightning Source LLC
Chambersburg PA
CBHW031527120626
46545CB00005B/2034